GOSPEL TRAILBLAZER

GOSPEL TRAILBLAZER
The Exciting Story of Francis Asbury

Bettie Wilson Story
ILLUSTRATED BY CHARLES COX

◆

ABINGDON PRESS
NASHVILLE

Gospel Trailblazer:
The Exciting Story of Francis Asbury

Copyright © 1984 by Bettie Wilson Story

Library of Congress Cataloging in Publication Data

STORY, BETTIE WILSON.
  Gospel trailblazer.
  Bibliography: p.
  Summary: A biography of Francis Asbury, first bishop of
the Methodist Church to be ordained in America.
  1. Asbury, Francis, 1745-1816—Juvenile literature.
  2. Methodist Church—United States—Bishops—
Biography—Juvenile literature. [1. Asbury, Francis,
1745-1816. 2. Methodist Church—Bishops. 3. Clergy]
I. Title
BX8495.A8S76   1984   287'.092'4 [B]   83-15032

ISBN-0-687-15652-1

MANUFACTURED BY THE PARTHENON PRESS AT
NASHVILLE, TENNESSEE, UNITED STATES OF AMERICA

for

G. L.

drawn by cords of love

Special thanks for their assistance to

Frederick A. Norwood
Professor Emeritus of History of Christianity,
Garrett-Evangelical Theological Seminary

Robert C. Bray,
Associate Professor of English,
Illinois Wesleyan University

Charles Merrill Smith,
minister, essayist, novelist

◆ CONTENTS ◆

GOSPEL TRAILBLAZER

CHAPTER 1

FROM THE DAY HE WAS BORN

◆

When Francis Asbury was born, his mother claimed he would become a great religious leader. God told her so in a dream while the baby was still in her womb, she said. As it turned out, her prediction was right. She would have been proud to hear the American President Calvin Coolidge praise her son more than a hundred years after his death. Unveiling a statue of Francis on horseback in the nation's capitol on October 15, 1924, the president said, "A great lesson has been taught us by this holy life."

But in August of 1745 in Handsworth Parish, England, where Francis was born, the idea was pure fantasy in a simple woman's mind.

For one thing, his parents were poor. Joseph, his father, did the best he could for the family. When he could no longer support them on the tiny farm near their modest cottage, he hired himself out as a gardener for the two wealthiest families in the parish. But everyone knew that religious leaders came only from the university-

11

educated upper class, not from lowly gardeners or farmers.

Moreover, it was not a happy time in England for children. Most of the poor were working by five years of age. If he were lucky, Francis might be placed in a wealthy home as a servant. Or he could be sent to the iron and brass foundries in nearby Birmingham to work from sunup to sundown. Surely his parents would save him from climbing to an early, dark death as a chimney sweep or being sent to work in the northern coal mines.

Elizabeth Asbury had other plans for her son. She had gone through a long, agonizing, barren time mourning the death of their young daughter, Sarah, who had died of a fever. Her guilt and grief had almost driven her out of her mind. She felt that God must be punishing her for some great sin by allowing Sarah to die. But, ah! The dream! It foretold that with the birth of a son, God would bless them. She could be humored for thinking that God meant Francis to be a future archbishop of Canterbury—the highest and most respected church position in all England. She would devote herself to his religious training.

How could her neighbors, who probably rolled their eyes and smiled when they heard Elizabeth tell about her dream from God, have guessed that Francis would learn early to stand firm for what he believed? That he would accept the call of the founder of Methodism, John Wesley, to go to America as a missionary? That although his formal education was meager, he taught himself to read the Bible in Greek, Hebrew, and Latin? That he would become the best known man in America in his day, the first bishop of the Methodist Church ordained in America?

The discipline and dedication of Francis to God began as an infant with the strict religious devotion of his mother. From the time he was born she read the Bible to him for an hour each day. She spent another hour with him in prayer and singing hymns written by Charles Wesley and by Isaac Watts—hymns that weren't the most reassuring lullabies for an infant:

> Alas! And did my Savior bleed
> And did my Sovereign die?
> Would he devote that sacred head
> For such a worm as I?

Francis was hardly old enough to sit alone when his mother taught him how to hold his hands in prayer. When she invited religious groups and classes into her house, possibly some Methodists, she must have held him in her arms to hear the devotions and prayers of people who wanted to live a holy life.

If he ever dreamed of rebelling from his early training, he would tell no one. For one thing, it would break his mother's heart. On top of Sarah's death, he would not dare add to his mother's sadness; he cared for her too much. Watching her affected him deeply although he could not talk about it. She would sit for hours by the window to read and pray or weep over her daughter's death.

If anything went wrong with Francis, she might consider it another visitation of God's wrath. That was unthinkable for a mother who opened "her house, her heart to receive the people of God and the ministers of Christ," as her son later described her.

What's more, Francis was taught the popular view that children were born in total wickedness. To avoid God's anger children must always be on their best behavior. Even minor offenses, idleness, for instance, could bring them "everlasting punishment" after they died. It was terrifying to a timid, sad child like Francis.

All he wanted to do, he admitted later, was to "do good and get good." And the way to do that was to be as devoted as his mother. He would be the kind of boy who pleased a revengeful God. He would not lie, fight, swear, and be "lighthearted" as other boys. Surely an angry God would despise play and laughter, so Francis avoided these. It seemed not to matter that children heckled him and called him Methodist parson, because of his serious nature, but he did not change his ways. He probably heard plenty of people in the village whispering about his parents, ridiculing them for the religious fanatics his mother invited into their home. He watched the visitors in his house pray and read the Bible for long hours, sing hymns, and cry over their sins. But being emotional in England was frowned upon, and "Methodist" was a contemptible name.

Neither were those the times for laughter. Morals in England were low. Drunkenness was a national disaster. Most of the deaths in London were children under five years old. Evils of the age included cardplaying for high gambling stakes, theft, cock fights, wrestling, Sabbath breaking, sexual abuse and adultery, and smuggling in port cities along the coast. In the midst of the extreme wealth of a few people, the great majority lived in rags on the streets of London and throughout the countryside.

Into these sad times came John and Charles Wesley and other Methodists and religious groups that gave hope to the poor. Many of these people feared God's wrath; they also believed in a real Satan who was leading them to a fiery hell. And God had already decided, they thought, who would be saved from these horrors after death. There was nothing they could do about it.

The Wesleys, however, talked about a personal faith in Christ who loved all people and who was reaching out to them. Love was most important and God's love was for everyone, even the poor and down-and-out in English society, if they would accept him and turn from their evil ways.

Members of the Methodist societies were people who believed God had forgiven them for their past life, so they gave up personal habits they decided were wrong for a Christian to have. They tried to ignore the sneers of old friends they had associated with before they were "saved." Yet pride over this confidence in God's forgiveness was one of the temptations they must avoid. God could see their every act, and they were not free from temptations. So they needed strict rules for their daily lives; for they believed they could, by their behavior and faith, work toward perfection.

Seeing religious groups in his home was as natural to Francis as breathing. At the same time his mother, with no great education, taught him to read the Bible by the time he was six. And his father, who would make any sacrifice for him, was arranging for his formal education. He sent him to Snail's Green, less than two miles over the rolling countryside from home. There Francis was most likely taught "piety" and the three Rs—reading, writing, and arithmetic.

School was a disaster. Fear raged in him because of the cruel beatings of the headmaster. What sin had he done to deserve such cruelty? he wondered. It drove him to prayer. In fact, he prayed right in the classroom, which only made the master beat him harder. God might be punishing him, he thought, but the headmaster filled him "with such horrible dread that with me anything was preferable to going to school."

The other boys could stay there and endure the abuse, but he would not. No education was that important. How dreadfully sad, however, for him to disappoint his parents who planned for Francis to get a good education. Under the circumstances they knew nothing else to do but to remove him from Snail's Green. It must have been the only place where a poor boy in the countryside could go to school, or they would have found another one for him.

The village people no doubt shrugged. School was not held in high regard by a majority of simple, ordinary folks anyway. Compared to working, going to school was idleness. The "easy life" might discourage one when grown up from sober, "downright labor." The village neighbors no doubt thought it better that Joseph Asbury place his son in a wealthy home. At least there he could earn his keep. After leaving Snail's Green, therefore, seven-year-old Francis spent a year in a prosperous home, probably working as a servant.

Certain apprenticeships gave children training for a special trade such as Francis was seeking. More often, however, masters exploited the children for cheap labor. They would receive food and shelter but no pay in exchange for long daily hours of work. They were treated as servants.

Abuses by the master were common. If he did not need a child for the full seven years of the apprenticeship, or if his fortunes changed so that he could no longer feed or clothe the apprentice, he might sell him to another master. He might even beat him severely and starve him or turn him out on the streets to beg and steal and bring each day's loot back to the master.

When he was thirteen Francis moved into a home as an apprentice. There he would learn a trade for several years and then be on his own to make his way in the world. He was lucky that the family treated him well. "I enjoyed great liberty," he reported, "and in the family was treated more like a son and an equal than apprentice."

It is popularly accepted that his apprenticeship was with a blacksmith named Foxall, who also was a Methodist, but Francis did not say so. He may have worked at brass button or buckle making. Although little is known of his almost seven years there, the care and love in the family must have banished some of his childhood fears. During this time his work was necessary but not important to him. The consuming passion for religion in his early home life was lying dormant, waiting for an outlet.

He had begun his apprenticeship only a short time before "God sent a pious man, not a Methodist, into our neighborhood, and my mother invited him to our house; by his conversation and prayers, I was awakened before I was fourteen years of age. . . . I began to pray morning and evening, being drawn by the cords of love."

Later, when he again visited his parents he asked his mother a question that would start him on the single-minded path toward fulfillment of her vision from God. "Who, where, and what were the Methodists: she gave me a favorable account, and directed me to a person that could take me to . . . hear them."

CHAPTER 2

ANSWERING THE CALL

♦

In the 1760s life for Francis Asbury and his country seemed to be getting better. Britain had won out over France in a war for the control of Canada. Hopes were raised with the crowning of their twenty-two-year-old king, George III. A strong reaction to corruption was growing. And ordinary, troubled people were finding a new hope and purpose in a personal religion.

These zealous people were not leaving the Church of England. They attended worship and received the holy sacraments in the established church, to which they also paid taxes. Their class meetings, "bands," love feasts, and prayer meetings were held at other times in the church parish. John Wesley, Methodism's founder and leader, remained a clergyman in the Church of England all his life. However, he and others were often barred from preaching in the church. Although others raised the question, Wesley would not admit that Methodism, which began as a reform movement within the church, would ever completely separate from it.

The Asburys were also members of the Church of England, but more important to them were the religious groups outside the church that they invited into their cottage for meetings. Elizabeth no doubt was pleased when her son asked about the Methodists. She put him in touch with a group in Wednesbury, north of Birmingham. In years past mobs in the town had fiercely persecuted the Methodists, as well as John Wesley when he came to preach. But by the time Francis heard the enthusiastic preaching of John Fletcher and Benjamin Ingham, the parish had a strong Methodist group.

"The people were so devout—men and women kneeling down—saying *Amen.* Now, behold! they were singing hymns—sweet sound!" Francis reported. "Why, strange to tell! the preacher had no prayerbook, and yet he prayed wonderfully! What was yet more extraordinary, the man took his text, and had no sermon book: thought I, *This is wonderful indeed! It is certainly a strange way, but the best way.*"

That kind of devotion suited Francis. He could not stay away from meetings, often attending as many as five a week, either at five o'clock in the morning or in the evening after work. They met for reading and prayer and "were much persecuted until the persons at whose houses we held them were afraid, and they were discontinued." He then held meetings frequently at his father's house.

The Methodists had just the kind of rules for conduct that Francis was looking for. Living by them showed one's devotion to God. And despite his limited education, wonder of wonders: The class meetings gave him the chance to lead in prayer and Bible reading. His mother gave him even more opportunities for this.

She took him to a women's meeting every two weeks where he often led the singing, prayed, or read the Bible and talked to the group about how they could live the way the Bible taught.

He could not be an Oxford University educated minister in the Church of England, as was his model John Wesley, but by age eighteen he could exclaim: "Behold me now a local preacher!—the humble and willing servant of any and of every preacher that called on me by night or by day; being ready, with hasty steps, to go far and wide to do good, visiting . . . almost every place within my reach, for the sake of precious souls; preaching, generally, three, four, and five times a week, and at the same time pursuing my calling."

On August 18, 1767, just before his twenty-second birthday, he gave up his secular work and was admitted on a trial basis as one of John Wesley's appointed full-time "traveling preachers." Although sent to particular parishes, Methodists preached anywhere they could draw a group around them—in open fields, in barns or homes, on street corners, in the village market squares, and even in the mines.

Because John Wesley needed so many to spread the Methodist gospel throughout England, he appointed several, like Francis, who did not have advanced education. But he expected them to study and read regularly. To aid them, he provided many materials, including the Bible, pamphlets, books, and sermons, many of which he had written.

Francis, often feeling inadequate over his lack of formal schooling, had "his nose in a book" wherever he traveled. Not even long hours on horseback hindered him. This was a habit picked up from John Wesley. In later years Francis complained that Wesley had it better in England; the roads and trails in America were too rugged for much reading. But people loved to tell the story, whether or not it really happened, of how Francis was so absorbed in a book that he rode his horse unawares right between the British and American lines during the Revolution. It was not until the next day, they claimed, that he discovered a bullet hole in his hat. The story supported their view that he would finish whatever he set out to do, regardless of what was going on around him.

Being an uneducated traveling preacher in England during the 1760s was not easy. The priest of the local parish Church of England might organize some of his members to run the preacher out of town. Rough miners, who could not remember the last time they had gone to church, might take offense at sermons and beat him up. Or mobs might ridicule him as if he were "strange and freakish." After all, those Methodists distrusted all amusement; they were hard workers, and they preached against drunkenness and other temptations "of the flesh."

Francis interpreted hardships as signs that he was obeying God's will. But in a July 20, 1770, letter from Bedfordshire to his parents, he showed that the persecution could weigh him down: "I despair almost of holding out to the end, when I think of the difficulties I have to wade through. . . . At this time I am in trying circumstances about the people and places; but sometimes I please myself that I shall . . . leave these parts."

Wherever he went he knew his sensitivity to suffering would go with him. Moreover, "the devil will be hard at my heels to tempt me; and if my trials are different, still they will and must come."

Between 1767 and 1771 he served the circuits of Bedfordshire, Essex, and South Wiltshire. Perhaps John Wesley thought it was only youthful eagerness that drew Francis to other circuits on occasion to preach and to lead class meetings. Those circuits were assigned by Wesley to others. He told Francis to stay "where he was put" and not "ramble all around." That was impossible; Francis seemed driven to ramble.

After the strict training of his childhood, his single-hearted attention to his work should have surprised his mother least of all. She did not quarrel with God over her son's calling, but was it necessary for him to be gone all the time? Didn't she and her husband deserve to see him more often?

He tried to be sensitive to her feelings. "Why will you mourn in such a manner?" he wrote her. "If you have given me to the Lord let it be a free will offering, and don't grieve for me. I have cause to be thankful that such a poor, ignorant, foolish, unfaithful, unfruitful creature should be called to the work. . . . I trust you will be easy and more quiet."

She could not. He was her only son.

"I do not expect to stay here another year," he told his parents in mid-1770. Perhaps even then his mind was rambling to a faraway place—to America. Was God calling him there?

America was much on the public mind. George III, welcomed to the British throne a few years before, was not popular in the colonies. For one thing, he had decided to tax the colonies to help pay for Britain's enormous war debt. He tried several ways to do this. One was the Sugar Act, but merchants got around it by smuggling along the New England coast. The Stamp Act lasted only a year. Others that could not be enforced were also repealed—leaving on the books only the hated tea tax.

At that time Francis was so taken up with his missionary zeal that he paid no attention to political rumblings; but he obviously paid attention to his restless curiosity about the colonies. Then in 1771 he attended his first annual conference of Methodist preachers, held in Bristol. He knew that John Wesley had spread Methodism throughout England and Scotland and every county in Ireland. A few Methodists had even

25

emigrated from Ireland to America and set up class meetings and societies in the New World.

These Methodists had written Wesley that they were buying preaching houses in America. They needed help. Wesley had sent over two missionaries in 1769, Joseph Pilmore and Richard Boardman. Now he needed to send more. He issued the challenge:

"Our brothers in America call aloud for help. Who are willing to go over and help them?" he asked more than a hundred preachers attending the Bristol conference.

Francis could not resist the challenge. About two million people lived in America. They needed to turn to Christ and take up the rules of the Methodist faith. Out of five volunteers, he and Richard Wright were selected.

John Wesley judged that Francis had a call from God to go to America. It was a call Francis never doubted. But first he must go home and gently break the news to his parents.

◆ CHAPTER 3 ◆

BOUND TO THE NEW WORLD

◆

The voyage to America, which began from Bristol on September 4, 1771, was anything but pleasant. "No sickness I ever knew was equal to" the seasickness Francis experienced the first three days on the square rigger. Gale winds blew off and on throughout the seven-week voyage to make the wooden ship "turn up and down and from side to side," he wrote in a journal he began to keep at the start of the journey.

Moreover, he had not brought a bed so he slept on a couple of blankets. He might as well have had nothing between him and the hard boards. He didn't have any privacy on the crowded ship, and food was in short supply. "Surrounded with men and women ignorant of God, and very wicked," he preached to them several times on deck. As far as he could tell, he did not change any listeners. He tried hard enough, even fixed his back against the mizzenmast so he could preach during a mighty wind one Sunday. But he got no response from anyone, certainly not the weathered sailors standing high on the footropes to adjust the square canvas sails.

No wonder he began to ask why he was heading to the New World. Where was he going? What was he to do? "I am going to live to God, and to bring others so to do," he answered.

Possibly to cheer himself he recalled the work of the Methodists in England. "The doctrine they preach, and the discipline they enforce are, I believe, the purest of any people now in the world." God had blessed the Methodists, and so he must be pleased with their beliefs and rules.

Among the books he had brought with him, Francis read the Bible, Mr. Wesley's sermons, and *Pilgrim's Progress*. He began to "feel my spirit bound to the New World, and my heart united to the people, though unknown. . . . I have the cause of God at heart." As the ship neared shore, its flags flying high on the masts, his chest swelled as if it would burst. He could hardly wait to preach to the people.

When the ship docked up the Delaware River at Philadelphia on October 27, Francis and Richard Wright contacted immediately a family who often entertained preachers. And that night, guided by the city's famous street lamps, which burned whale oil, they went to St. George's Church to hear Joseph Pilmore preach. Francis was overwhelmed by the affection the large congregation showered on him and Wright.

Francis wasted no time. He did not seem to notice the neat brick houses with white trim. Or perhaps the woman wearing a big apron and calico cap who was sweeping her porch as he passed. Or the gables and cupola of Carpenters' Hall, where the first Continental Congress would meet in three years. He must preach. And he went straight back to St. George's Church the next day to do so.

His brown hair fell to his shoulders; his nose was sharp, his forehead high. But his most distinguishing feature was his eyes. Their blue intensity gave urgency to his sermon. They seemed to say that he would soon be traveling on.

When the time came in less than a week, however, he did not wish to leave Philadelphia, the second largest city in the British Empire—second only to London. The people had opened their hearts to him, and God was with them, he said. But he needed to travel to the next largest city in the colonies, New York, in the lower tip of Manhattan Island. Richard Boardman was there, and as John Wesley's assistant, he was in charge of assigning traveling preachers to their circuits.

Unlike Philadelphia with its neat, clean houses and walks and its own garbage collection, New York's narrow streets were formed simply where people or cows wore paths. Pigs roamed freely in the filthy streets, and good drinking water was available only from hawkers with their horse-drawn carts.

Boardman assigned the newcomer to New York. But within less than a week after his arrival, Francis was ready to move out. It was not because of the people at Wesley Chapel on John Street; they were friendly and many seemed to have a love of discipline. This would endear them especially to the new preacher who lived each day by strict Methodist rules he learned from John Wesley.

It was not because of Boardman's personality. He was a friendly man, kind and entertaining, Francis thought. It was not because of the conditions in town; he had no time to fret over his physical surroundings.

Francis simply was chafing to get on the road. Most of the two and a quarter million people in America lived in the country, within a hundred miles of the Atlantic coast. With only twenty thousand residents, New York certainly did not need two Methodist preachers. He had to keep reminding himself that he would be fixed to the Methodist plan. That plan, according to his superior, Boardman, called for him to remain in the city.

But preachers in England were itinerants, or travelers. They stayed on the move to reach people with their message of God's love for everyone. Francis was on fire with the Methodist belief that if people did not ask forgiveness of their sins from God and change their ways, they were headed for a hell of horrors and eternal damnation. The time was now. The message was urgent. The rules to live by were needed. Everyone must be reached. Other preachers might wish to stay "shut up in the cities all winter, but I think I shall show them the way," he said.

Even though he did not have permission, he set out with a couple of trustees of Wesley Chapel (later named John Street Church) who often traveled with preachers. Their destination was Westchester, about twenty miles north of town. At the courthouse and in surrounding areas such as West Farms, Francis preached on familiar Methodist revival themes: Repent of your sins, believe in Jesus, love one another.

By early December he was back in New York. When he discovered Boardman was still in town, he decided to mount his horse again for Westchester, then on to Eastchester, New Rochelle, and the manor home of Frederick Deveau. There he preached for the family, their large company of servants, and neighbors. Deveau was a good friend who opened his home to Methodists at every opportunity. Francis then set off to Rye, New York, and backtracked to all of his first stops, preaching at each one. By the end of the month he had a "great pain in the head" and was severely ill.

Thus his first weeks in America established a pattern that was to stay with him for the next forty-five years—constant travel with almost daily preaching, strict personal discipline, and painful illnesses that brought him close to death more than once. In late January and February of 1772, after scarcely three months in the new land, he had pushed himself too far in the harsh winter. He finally was forced to stay in bed several days. "Surely God has sent me to these people," he wrote. Many had not heard the gospel preached for more than a year until he traveled among them. His weak body would have to adjust to his traveling spirit and his one mission for God.

The twenty-six year old upstart, Francis, was in disagreement with the two older missionaries from the beginning about traveling assignments. He determined that he would stand steadfast as a wall of brass, as he put it, on this issue. Nothing was more displeasing to Joseph Pilmore than having to move to another place. But Francis finally influenced Boardman enough that he decided to reappoint preachers every three months. Boardman went to Boston, Pilmore to Virginia, where the Church of England and Methodists were strong, and Richard Wright to New York.

Francis was delighted in April to be assigned to Philadelphia, although he would not limit himself to its boundaries very long. Within less than a week, he was traveling out from Philadelphia into Bohemia (Cecil County, Maryland), to Chester, and casting his eye toward Baltimore, ninety miles away. The circuit also included New Jersey.

"I humbly hope, before long," Francis reported, that "about seven preachers of us will spread seven or eight hundred miles, and preach in as many places as we are able to attend." He would accept no boundaries for the Methodist missionary.

The colonies were far from united, although they did not hamper people in traveling from one to another. Each colony had separate currency, militia, and governments. Roads for wagons or carriages hardly existed; they were horse paths and Indian trails. Most people, however, traveled less than forty miles from home.

The Methodists in America related to the Church of England the same way they did in Britain. Members went to the church to receive the sacrament of Holy Communion and were a part of the church parish. The problem was that there were few parishes in America and not enough parish priests to serve all the Methodists. Also most established-church priests did not want Methodist preachers to work in their parishes; they had no need of assistants, they said. Furthermore, they had no use for uneducated lay preachers. Not a single Methodist preacher in America was ordained.

Francis felt comfortable with the Wesley plan; if people wanted Holy Communion they could go to the established church. He was totally opposed, however, to himself or any other lay preacher serving the sacraments; they did not have approval to do so by church law.

There were other preachers who had begun the Methodist movement five years earlier in America. They had worked independently of John Wesley until he sent over the first missionaries, Pilmore and Boardman. Two were Philip Embury and Robert Strawbridge, lay preachers who had come from societies in Ireland. There was also Captain Thomas Webb, who had served British military duty in America, and now was back as a preacher.

Francis soon found out, possibly from Robert Williams, another Irishman who had come over in 1769 and was preaching in Virginia, that the issue of Holy Communion was not as simple as he thought. Preachers had gotten pretty hot about it in the South, particularly Robert Strawbridge who worked according to his own rules. He did not take a regular assignment under Boardman after he arrived as Wesley's assistant, but worked primarily in Maryland and Virginia on his own. Strawbridge was violating the rules against baptizing people and serving them Holy Communion. But he did it all the time and no one was going to stop him, not even Wesley. Better to have the sacraments from him than from some immoral Church of England priest, he said.

Although Francis strongly held to the Methodist plan, he tried to play down the controversy. Holy Communion was not that important, he said. One could do without it. More important were turning to Christ and living right, which would send one out to win others to Christ.

Perhaps Francis did not know that tensions were mounting in the southern colonies like Virginia over the British tax to support the Church of England. If Methodists were connected to the parishes, having to attend their services to receive the sacraments, wouldn't they be caught up in the struggle? And no one, least of all Methodists who stressed upright behavior, could approve the low moral standards of some of the parish priests.

The political tensions that were mounting between the colonies and Britain were not helping. What would happen to the Methodists and their relationship both to the established church and to John Wesley if America split away from England?

Would it tear apart the Methodist revival before it barely had a foothold in the colonies?

Francis would not let himself dwell on such an awful possibility. But his underlying concerns must have added to the emotional distress he suffered toward the end of his first year in the New World.

◆ C H A P T E R 4 ◆

STORM CLOUDS OF REVOLUTION

◆

Francis Asbury was losing his family. By the fall of 1772 his mother Elizabeth wrote begging him to come back to England. She was weak and wanted to see her only son again. Surely God could not deny a faithful mother that one wish.

But it was too late to change her son's nature. Perhaps, he wrote, he could return in a couple of years, but he had barely arrived in America. He took it for granted that his parents would not want him to "leave the work God has called me to, for the dearest friend in life." He expected that they would continue to support the preaching at home and to "stir up the people to meet together," which seemed to be their calling. Their love for one another on the other hand was not limited by the distance between them.

He wanted to hear from his parents. He often complained of how few letters he received from them. Friends traveling back and forth to England would bring him news of his parents, but it was scanty. In a two-year period he received only two letters from them and none at all for seven years during the Revolution.

Yet he could not admit that his father's prediction might come true. Standing at the dock in Bristol, Mr. Asbury had mournfully watched his son leave for America. With tears streaming down his face, he said, "We will never see him again." And they did not. Francis would show his devotion to them in other ways: writing them, sending them supporting funds out of his meager income, living the plain, pure life they had taught him. But he never returned home. He would have a great deal of anxiety for his "disobedient absence," he told them, if he did not have "superior obligations to my Heavenly Father."

Another fact was becoming clear—Francis was losing his country. He could feel it in his bones. Sooner or later a break with Britain would come. He met with friends from home and talked about their own country, and with a note of homesickness he wrote his parents, "Still old England for me!" But he could hear clamors against "old England" growing stronger. Methodists were right in the middle of the brewing storm. Among them were both Patriots and Tories, or Loyalists; those who were loyal to King George III.

Outsiders believed all of the thousand or so Methodists in the colonies were Loyalists even if they were born in America. Neighbors were dividing against neighbors. The Sons of Liberty, a terrorist group that had several names, were making raids on Loyalists. Other Patriots joined the Sons of Liberty to scare Loyalists into joining the Patriots or be run out of the country. Many Loyalists fled to the "back country" farther west or to Nova Scotia in Canada or home to Britain. Would England be wise in dealing with the colonies? Francis had his doubts.

"I fear the storm is gathering, and the cloud will break on my dear countrymen," he wrote his parents. A poor, unhappy man had even abused him on the road one October day in 1772: "He cursed, swore, and threw stones at me." The assailant could have simply been lashing out at the preacher, since most people were hostile to religion. Given the growing excitement against Britain, however, he may have judged Francis to be a Loyalist. Opposition was rising against both the Church of England and Methodist ministers for this reason. They increasingly received threats—they were beaten, they were tarred and feathered, they were even imprisoned.

Politics held no importance for someone as single-minded as Francis. "I must go on and mind my own business, which is enough for me, and leave all those things to the providence of God," he said.

That didn't keep him from being afraid or from being concerned for the colonies, the Methodists, and England. He suffered with his friends and tried to help. Returning to Baltimore in early 1774, he discovered that the widow Triplett, who opened her house regularly for Methodist meetings, had been the victim of a riot at her home. Francis advised her to file a complaint with the local magistrate. When the magistrate told her she would simply have to put up with the harassment, inferring that the laws did not protect supposed Loyalists, her friends were furious. Members of the Methodist society kept pouring in to vent their feelings at a called meeting on one Friday evening at William Moore's home.

Francis read to the group a pamphlet by John Wesley called the "Plain Account of the People Called Methodists." He told them, "We are a united body and will defend our own cause. . . . I have a legal right to preach the gospel." He went on to say that he had qualified himself according to the Act of Toleration. The act, passed by the Maryland Assembly, protected anyone who claimed to believe in Jesus Christ. Methodists qualified for protection whether or not they were Loyalists but did not always receive it.

If he were gradually losing a country, Francis had mixed feelings about the new country he was adopting. "I have seen enough to make me sick; . . . Americans are more willing to hear than to do; . . . but I am under Mr. Wesley's direction; and as he is a father and friend, I hope I shall never turn my back on him," he wrote his parents.

There was much poverty in the towns. England had dumped convicted criminals by the thousands from their prisons into Maryland and other middle colonies. In the villages and on the farms life was hard, full of danger, and lonely. Slavery carried its own tragedies both in the North and the South. Most of the people were weary of fighting the wilderness and frightened at the thought of revolution.

At the same time, anyone who enforced John Wesley's strict rules of conduct in such a loose culture could expect opposition. While Francis wanted everyone to be caught up in God's love, he was as strict as Wesley in that people must prove themselves to be members of a Methodist society. Thousands could come hear him preach, but belonging to a small class meeting or society was another matter. "We will have a holy people or none," he said.

Being holy, according to Wesley's rules, included no dancing, cardplaying, laziness, light foolish talk or evil speech of anyone, no fancy clothes with ornaments or ruffles, jewelry or laces, colored waistcoats, or costly buttons and buckles (Methodists in America were often mistaken for Quakers). Neither did Wesley wish anyone to marry outside the Methodist membership. Members were to be on time for everything and were to spend part of every day in prayer, meditation, and Bible reading.

Francis would bar from society meetings those who did not conform to the discipline. He did not want to have any "half-hearted Methodists" who might distract the others. Some members of the New York society got so upset over this strictness that they wanted to ban him from their midst. That didn't disturb him at all. He knew he was right. If Francis had not possessed a personal enthusiasm that was inspiring, plus a natural wit and good sense, they would have ridden him out of town on his saddlebags.

As if he were looking far into the future, for the first time he realized he was at the mercy of the people. ". . . Though I consider sometimes I am here in a strange land, nothing to depend on but the kindness of friends, am spending the best of my days, what shall I do when I am old?"

He would have to trust in the Lord because he certainly would not change his ways. In the years to come he had no desire or time to prepare for his old age. All his life he simply stayed with friends or strangers or rented a room if turned away from someone's home. He stayed with the wealthy and the poor alike, or slept in the open forest, even in jails if he had no other place. He never had a home of his own, but the time did come when he kept a few personal belongings—books, a saddlebag, an extra shirt—in an attic room at the home of the preacher of the Light Street Church in Baltimore.

"Where are you from?" someone asked once as he journeyed in Ohio.

"From Boston, New York, Philadelphia, Baltimore, or almost any place you please," Francis answered. That was no tall tale.

Francis was also losing his health. Between the summer of 1773 and the end of the year, he was ill more than a third of the time. Friends often wept at his bedside in fear that he was dying. Indeed, he was so sick that he sometimes expected death or wished for it. Colds, coughs, swelling, high fevers, severe headaches, back and neck pains, ulcers in his throat and stomach, and many other problems plagued him.

Always impatient to be on the road, he would often travel with a fever, then preach and go to bed. Sometimes he stayed several days with a family because he was too sick to leave. Other times he moved on against the advice of friends, disregarding his fatigue. If he did not have long to live, he must "do all the good" he could in the time he had.

In addition, he was extremely critical of his own holy life. He always wearied "of all the wrong that is in me," always upbraiding himself if he got a tinge of pride or expressed humor or received praise. When depressed over his health, he would often turn on himself. He was unfaithful to God, too impatient, self-pleasing, and discontented, he thought. "My body was very weak. . . . If I am the Lord's, why am I thus?" he would plead. In the next breath he would decide his afflictions must be needed to make him a better servant of God.

Yet his body, over medium height and slender, was also quite strong to survive his schedule despite heat or cold, rain or sun, or condition of the trail.

In late 1772, John Wesley sent word from England that he had appointed Francis as his assistant. This put him in charge of the Methodist work in America, replacing William Boardman and making him responsible for the assignments of preachers. He set out to visit all the circuits to check their work. Despite his other concerns of health, family, and political tensions, this responsibility weighed heavily on him.

By late November he was in the deepest melancholy of his life. "My mind was greatly depressed . . . partly from the state of my body, and partly from a deep sense of the very great work in which I am employed. I do not know when I sunk into deeper distress."

By the early summer of the next year, when Wesley sent Thomas Rankin and George Shadford to America, Francis looked back on the past ten months of ill health and decided he had not done too badly. He had ridden two thousand miles on horseback, primarily in Maryland and Delaware, frequently with a high fever, and had preached three hundred times.

How difficult it was for him to be silent or to stay in one place. The Revolution would bring another confinement, which to a rambling preacher seemed like a prison.

◆ CHAPTER 5 ◆

A DIVIDED PEOPLE

From the time Thomas Rankin and George Shadford arrived from England in mid-1773, any friendship between Rankin and Francis seemed doomed to failure. John Wesley had named Rankin to replace Francis as assistant. This placed Rankin in charge of all the preachers and societies. Granted, Francis sometimes felt inadequate as assistant. He had tried to convince Wesley more than once to come to America. Instead Wesley sent over another preacher just as strong willed as Francis.

Rankin had a lot of talent and was a good man, but Francis thought he decided too many things that should have been decided by all the preachers. One thing Francis respected was the way Rankin demanded strict discipline, but he didn't have to be so hardheaded about it. He was brand-new on the continent, and he wasn't even considering the views and wishes of the people. He absolutely could not understand why anybody would be opposed to King George III. The

Boston Tea Party, staged by the Sons of Liberty, and other guerrilla activities alarmed him enough that in less than a year, he was already wondering if all the missionaries should return to England. Boardman and Pilmore did return in 1774 due to political tensions.

For the five years that Rankin stayed in America, he and Francis disagreed with each other on a regular basis. Francis grumbled over the preaching assignments Rankin gave him. He wanted to go to Baltimore, but Rankin sent him first to New York, then Philadelphia. Each wrote John Wesley complaining of the other. Once Wesley went so far as to write Rankin to send Francis back to England, but it was never pushed. Francis certainly would have refused.

In 1775 Francis got his first trip into Virginia when Rankin appointed him to Norfolk, the largest town in that colony. Arriving by boat he saw first the port established for the tobacco fleet, a man-of-war in the harbor, and warehouses lining the docks. He also found thirty Methodists who worshiped in an "old, shattered playhouse"; he cut the membership down to fourteen because some were disobeying Wesley's rules. Then he divided his time between Portsmouth and Norfolk and rode horseback to preach and organize societies throughout the parish and into the swamps toward the North Carolina border. Sometimes guards or committees investigating traveling strangers stopped him, a stark reminder that the war had gotten more serious after the Battle of Bunker Hill near Boston. Lord Dunmore, British

governor of Virginia, had fled that year to a British ship. While Francis was traveling over the countryside along the Virginia coast, militia were moving in the south and Lord Dunmore had a fleet in Chesapeake Bay, which was raiding the coast. By the time he and his Loyalist recruits burned the town of Norfolk on New Year's Day, 1776, Francis was already on his way back to Philadelphia.

Earlier Francis had been stunned by a letter from Thomas Rankin stating that he and two others had decided it would be better to return to England.

"It would be an eternal dishonor to the Methodists," Francis wrote in his journal, "that we should all leave three thousand souls, who desire to commit themselves to our care; neither is it the part of a good shepherd to leave his flock in time of danger; therefore, I am determined, by the grace of God, not to leave them, let the consequence be what it may."

He wrote the same to Rankin. It was evidently so strongly worded that it shamed Rankin into changing his mind to stay.

In contrast, George Shadford and Francis became close friends. Francis accounted for every minute of his time and constantly judged himself on how well it was spent in God's work. Yet his friendship with Shadford was so strong that they could spend a full day enjoying conversation together without Francis blaming himself for being idle.

By 1776 the war was in full force although most

of it was taking place in New England. Patriots throughout the colonies, however, conducted terrorist raids against Loyalists. Native-born Methodist preachers like William Watters and Freeborn Garrettson were even ill-treated as suspected Loyalists. Garrettson was almost beaten to death.

How much more were the English preachers under suspicion. They were not helped any by John Wesley who issued his "Calm Address to our American Colonies." Wesley's opposition to the Revolution infuriated Patriots and their sympathizers. Francis thought the "venerable father" should have stayed away from American politics. People used Wesley's political views, he said, as an excuse to censure Methodists in America.

It was certainly a civil war of terrible atrocities by Patriots and Loyalists against one another. Only one third of the colonists backed the Revolution. Not that they had much choice— voters must be men with property; the poor, women, and blacks had no voice in government at any level. The merchants, landed gentry, and politicians were the most disturbed over British rule.

Others reacted in various ways. Some fifty thousand Americans joined the British troops. New England farmers sold food to both sides, but especially to the British because they paid in hard currency, not worthless "Continental" paper money. "Outliers" mostly from the Carolinas left families at home and hid out to avoid taking allegiance to the king. Both Patriots and Loyalists

who had political enemies fled to safer ground—
"over the mountain" to Tennessee or to Canada.
Freedom of the press and free speech were only
for Patriots, and one hundred thousand Loyalists
left America during the Revolution because mobs
attacked them or stripped away their property.
Others stayed and formed their own terrorist
groups. Many tried to live peacefully and survive
until the war would end. And while the militia,
the Continental Army, the British Redcoats, the
navies, and politicians moved up and down the
eastern seaboard, there were several Methodist
preachers traveling up and down the seaboard
too, trying to spread "scriptural holiness" through
abnormal, trying times.

The people were distracted by the war; they
were not living up to Wesley's rules. They needed
to work for their own salvation, Francis said.
They needed a strong leader; he no doubt
expected to be that leader.

In addition, some Methodist preachers from
England were loudly opposing the Revolution, even
passing out pamphlets supporting the British cause.
The most damaging was Martin Rodda who finally
had to flee inside the British lines. Most preachers
tried to be like Francis in not coming out for either
side in the political strife. A few, like Thomas
Ware, enlisted with the Patriots.

New York fell to the British in late 1776, and
Philadelphia the next year. Philadelphia's occu-
pation ended in a few months, but New York's
control by the British cut off the Methodist

societies in that city from those in other colonies for five years.

Francis kept his hope. God has his way in the whirlwind, he said, so he could leave all the "little affairs of the world" and go about his proper business of "saving my own soul and those that hear me"—both Patriot and Loyalist.

Despite these stresses, who but a close friend could make Francis question his decision to stay in America? Perhaps he was forcing his will on God. If so, he would discover it when he and George Shadford came together for a day to fast and pray about what they ought to do. Afterward Francis felt God was telling him to stay in America, Shadford felt he was to go to England.

"One of us is wrong!" Francis said. His penetrating blue eyes gazed out from a grave face.

Shadford disagreed. Perhaps God wanted one to leave, one to stay. They both wept.

Shadford returned to England. So did Rankin. He slipped inside the British lines without so much as a farewell. By early 1778 all of the British missionaries had left for England or Canada. All except Francis Asbury. His decision to stay was probably one of the most important of his life.

He admitted his depression. "But it was no wonder: three thousand miles from home—my friends have left me—I am considered by some as an enemy of the country—every day liable to be seized by violence, and abused." He was a man without a country. Then he dismissed these hardships, "This is just a trifle to suffer for Christ. . . . Lord, stand by me!"

Out of sixty traveling preachers when Thomas Rankin called the first annual conference to meet in 1773, there were only twenty-eight five years later—all American born except one. War, death, and decisions to stop preaching due to physical hardships or marriage had reduced their number. None was ordained. Although John Wesley had not yet officially appointed him, Francis was once again the general assistant in America.

He had no time to adjust to the new situation as the only remaining British traveling preacher. The colonies with their different loyalty oaths were getting strict. To continue preaching in Maryland, Francis must sign an oath disclaiming allegiance to the king of England. In addition, the oath required the signer to defend the colony and to turn in names to authorities of any known enemies. Men between the ages of sixteen and sixty were being called into military service.

Francis would take an oath to no one but God. He would not bear arms. In the winter of 1778, when twenty-five hundred of General Washington's ragged troops were dying of starvation and exposure at Valley Forge, Francis left his beloved Baltimore and went into exile. His friend, Judge Thomas White, in Kent County near Dover, Delaware, sheltered him for two years.

Exile was no easy decision. The Methodist societies must be saved from collapse. Besides, nothing was more repugnant to him than staying cooped up in one place. "It requires great resignation for a man to be willing to be laid aside as a broken instrument," he said.

♦ C H A P T E R 6 ♦

THE EXILE

♦

Delaware had accepted the Declaration of Independence. But Loyalists, who were opposed to independence, were so strong that they elected a majority of their candidates to the colonial assembly in Dover and the united Continental Congress. Loyalists were selling supplies to the British and even fishing with the Redcoats along the shore! Loyalist judges would not convict other Loyalists of crimes, the Patriots accused. The atmosphere got so bitter that the Continental Congress sent in a Virginia regiment to avert violence during a Delaware election.

It was no wonder that Judge Thomas White came under suspicion when it was discovered he might be harboring a Methodist preacher. Had not the Methodist founder in England, John Wesley, denounced the American cause? Besides, a Tory hunt was going on. Brigadier General Caesar Rodney rounded up about twenty who were trading with the British and threw them in the Dover jail. A mob of Loyalists threatened to march on the town. They were beginning to lose the upper hand in the colony. Then Rodney took over as president of the Delaware Assembly.

Within a month after Francis arrived on the White farm, the judge was arrested for questioning on April 2, 1778. The family fled at this time, leaving Francis alone at the home. He decided that he should disappear for his safety and that of the Whites. He wandered from place to place in a swamp for two or three days, finally ending up at the home of John Fogwell in Queen Anne's County. The Whites returned right away, although their persecution continued for at least a year. Francis returned by the end of April. For the sake of his friends, he kept quiet, even if he did hate "dumb and silent Sabbaths" when he could not or was not allowed to preach.

He was sad to hear of the imprisonment of Methodist preachers in Maryland, but tried to resign himself to his own state of affairs. Perhaps God was telling him these were not the days to save souls when people were so filled with the troubles of the times. Once he almost decided to turn himself in to the authorities, but finally determined that it was "the will of God that I should be silent for a season to prepare me for further usefulness."

In that attitude he was as frugal with his time as ever, rising at four or five o'clock in the morning for prayer and meditation. He read the Bible in Hebrew and Greek, Wesley's works, and biographies. He studied medical books to help him treat his illnesses. He wrote letters. He prayed every hour for each preacher, calling each by name, a habit he had begun several years before. He improved his own spiritual life, which "had been in a degree neglected, on account of my great attention to the souls of others." He was happy with the family where he stayed and expressed wonder "at the love and care of Almighty God, towards such a dead dog as I am."

The season of silence might be good for him, but that did not mean he liked it. Melancholy set in; he needed activity to dispel it. Frequently he was also homesick for the English preachers. "I have no one to consult" without them, he moaned.

Exile could not hold him down for long. If he could not leave, what was to keep others from coming to him? Within a few weeks he began cautiously to hold family meetings at the White home; neighboring families came, too. Visitors began to drop by. He even got braver and held quarterly meetings of preachers and class leaders. By July he was visiting the sick and preaching, not only in Judge White's barn and house, but he was also venturing out to homes of neighbors. "I laid a plan for myself to travel and preach nine days in two weeks." This began to get him back on a regular schedule "in what appears to me as my duty, my element, and my delight!"

Meanwhile, General Washington chased after the British forces when General Clinton decided to abandon Philadelphia, which he had occupied for nine months. But the battle between them in Monmouth, New Jersey, on June 28, 1778, was indecisive. From then on the war took place between small fighting units on land and in naval battles at sea. The French joined its forces with America, and the hopes of the Patriots rose despite the British capture of Savannah, Georgia, in December.

In those same months of 1778 and 1779, Francis traveled out to preach and hold society and class meetings with Methodists in Delaware. He was able to reach many people. From thirty to seven hundred came to hear him, and he reported more than twelve hundred at quarterly meetings. Preachers wrote him letters; they came to see him at Judge White's home. He assigned them to circuits in the northern states despite limitations imposed on their work by the oaths and other regulations of each colony. He became a center of information for everything that was going on among Methodists in America.

One of the reasons he had increasingly more freedom to travel in Delaware was that one of his letters to Rankin in 1777 had been intercepted by authorities. Its content reduced suspicions of Francis as being sympathetic to the British. So he was able to leave Delaware for Maryland in April, 1780, after two years of confinement. The colony's president, Caesar Rodney, gave him a passport and letters of approval. No longer considered an enemy of the American cause, he still could not preach in Maryland.

He headed for the annual conference of northern preachers in Baltimore. Although he was delighted to see his Maryland friends once again, he "could not pray for our friends we left behind without weeping." During his semi-exile he had added eighteen hundred to the Methodist societies in Delaware; there were now about nine thousand members in all the colonies.

A primary concern that year was the heated controversy over whether or not preachers could serve Holy Communion to members. The year before, the northern preachers meeting with Francis at the home of Judge White had recognized Francis as John Wesley's assistant and voted to continue going to the Church of England for the sacraments. The southern preachers, on the other hand, voted their independence from Wesley's plan: they would ordain one another and provide the sacraments.

If there was anything Francis could not bear, it was the possibility of a split in the Methodist connection. Better for them not to have preachers at all than to be divided, he wrote Wesley. He had tried to get the southerners to change their minds through his letters from Delaware. Now he had the chance to persuade them in person.

But the northerners were not making it easy for Francis. They condemned the southern action and said that in order for union to take place, their brother ministers in the South must renounce what they had done.

Francis knew just how the southerners would react—they would reject the demands outright. He had no stomach to impose an iron will over the preachers. He needed to try another way to get what he wanted.

"A thought struck my mind," he said. Why not ask the southerners to suspend serving Holy Communion for a year until he could write John Wesley for guidance? For that year, the conferences could "cancel all . . . grievances, and be one."

Francis, Freeborn Garrettson, and William Watters headed south to "bring about peace and union." At the Fluvanna conference in Virginia on May 9, 1780, Francis addressed all sides of the issue and submitted his compromise proposal for a year's suspension of their former action. However, it was rejected.

Francis' hopes were crushed. "I then prepared to leave the house, to go to a near neighbor's to lodge, under the heaviest cloud I ever felt in America. O what I felt! . . . Nor I alone!—but the agents on both sides! They wept like children. . . ."

After praying all night in his room, he returned to the conference the next morning to give his farewell. The southerners began to tell him what had happened.

Their decision of the day before had broken their hearts, they said. So they changed their minds. They accepted the compromise. They would give Francis a year to write John Wesley for his suggestions.

Surely God's hand was in the decision, declared Francis. They immediately held a preaching service and a love feast. Again the people wept and prayed; this time it was with joy.

Francis did not head north. Instead he faced his horse in the direction of Petersburg to begin an almost six-month journey to all the circuits of Virginia and North Carolina. He would reunite the people and heal the divisions that had occurred over the sacraments controversy.

While he was in Petersburg the British captured Charleston, and soon all of South Carolina and Georgia were occupied by the Redcoats. The only victory for the Patriots that year was at King's Mountain, South Carolina, a bitter fight between frontiersmen and Loyalists. Only one non-American fought on either side.

Although John Wesley had made no decision on the sacraments by the time all the preachers in the colonies met in their annual conference of 1781, they supported Francis again on the issue.

But the most important event in 1781 was the defeat of the British General Cornwallis at Yorktown, Virginia. When he surrendered the Revolution ended. Francis did not make note of it in his journal. But even General George Washington expected more battles in the coming months. He did not count on everyone being sick of the war. After Yorktown, the British withdrew from the southern states and from New York.

John Wesley, meanwhile, was still pondering over what was needed for the Methodists in America. Something had to be done. He could not postpone a decision very long. The Church of England had as its head the British king. Crown authority could not continue in America after the peace treaty of 1783 severed America from the

British Empire. The church must reorganize. Where would the Methodists, who now numbered fourteen thousand and had no ordained ministers in America, go for Holy Communion and baptism?

The Revolution had cut off the colonies not only from the British government; it had separated them also from their religious roots.

◆ C H A P T E R 7 ◆

A BISHOP FOR A NEW CHURCH

Francis knew that John Wesley was sending three men from England to America in the fall of 1784: Thomas Coke, Richard Whatcoat, and Thomas Vasey. Imagine his shock when he discovered why they had come!

Mr. Wesley had found a way to ordain ministers in the new nation, Coke told him at Barrett's Chapel in Maryland on November 14. Wesley had already acted on a decision he thought he would never make—he had ordained Whatcoat and Vasey in England as ministers. Then he consecrated Coke as his superintendent and instructed him to ordain Francis and consecrate him as a superintendent. Thus the two of them, Coke and Francis, would be in charge of Methodism in America.

Coke had also brought along from Wesley a letter, rituals for different kinds of religious services, and Wesley's edition of the Thirty-nine Articles of Religion of the Church of England. Wesley had recognized the need to free his followers in America to make their own decisions about their future. But he would provide them with ordained leaders for their task. Who but Wesley as the father of Methodism should ordain its first ministers? He had decided that he was qualified to do so. But that decision was so controversial that he did not even share it with his brother, Charles.

Francis also had some qualms about the information. He had faced the possibility of a split among Methodists too long. He had worked too hard to hold the movement together. Nobody knew the people and societies as he did. And he respected the independent spirit of Americans. They would not accept him as their superintendent bishop just because Wesley said so. He would agree to it only if elected by the preachers.

The small group of preachers at the November 14 quarterly meeting talked about an independent church for the Methodists, and agreed with Francis to call a full conference of all preachers in America to plan their future. It would be held on December 24, 1784, at Lovely Lane Church, Baltimore. Freeborn Garrettson rode horseback more than twelve hundred miles in six weeks to let everyone know about it. About sixty of a total of more than eighty preachers attended.

The conference went on for ten days. They had gathered to ordain ministers and accept Wesley's plans, which had been brought over by Coke. While they were at it, they formed themselves into the Methodist Episcopal Church. How much easier they could carry out Wesley's plans as an organized church rather than a society in the Church of England!

They voted Thomas Coke and Francis Asbury as their superintendents, functioning as bishops. Francis began being called bishop right away because he used the term, but the title was not officially recorded in the minutes of the annual conferences until three years later.

Francis, who had been a lay traveling preacher for seventeen years, was ordained by Thomas Coke as deacon one day, elder the second, and consecrated superintendent on the third— December 27, 1784. He was thirty-nine years old. Assisting in the consecration was Philip William Otterbein, a German minister in Baltimore and close friend of Francis, and a founder of the Evangelical United Brethren Church. It would be almost one hundred and eighty-five years later (1968) before the churches of Asbury and Otterbein would join to form The United Methodist Church.

Twelve other preachers were ordained, including Freeborn Garrettson, who was sent to Nova Scotia in Canada to serve the Methodists and other Britishers who had fled during and after the Revolution.

The long arguments over the authority of unordained preachers to serve the Sacrament were over. Francis now could officially serve Communion and baptize members, and as superintendent he could ordain others to do so. John Wesley had recognized him for his work. He had the support and confidence of the people.

More importantly, the preachers had voted him in as their superintendent because he had already proved himself as a leader.

He had thought and prayed and fasted about Wesley's plan often in the five weeks between Coke's arrival and the Christmas Conference. "I am not tickled with the honor," he said, but he did finally conclude that it was within God's will. He wrote his parents simply, "I have seen the power of the Lord and expect to see greater things yet."

Now Methodists had their own church and their own clergy, with ritual and rules from Wesley, which were added to by members at the Christmas Conference. But they really did not know how to act as a church. So they went on about their work just as they had before as a society or sect. They would feel their way toward becoming a church just as the thirteen colonies would take up the task of trying to become a united nation.

Superintendents Coke and Francis would preside over the conferences and ordain and assign preachers to their traveling circuits. But that need not keep them in one place. The day after the historic Christmas Conference ended, Francis struck out for Virginia and North Carolina, traveling fifty miles the first day on horseback through ice and snow. He was doing what he loved best—crossing the countryside to preach and pray wherever he could pull together a group. It might be a gathering of thirty people, of one thousand, or even of one.

◆ CHAPTER 8 ◆

LIBERATION AND EDUCATION

Since Thomas Coke was going to share in the assignment of preachers to circuits, he needed to get acquainted with the men and the territory. He also needed to experience the kind of travel that Francis went through. So before the Christmas Conference, Francis sent him out on a nine-hundred-mile trip that he had just covered. Riding with Coke was Harry Hosier, a frequent traveling companion of Francis and the first black Methodist preacher in America.

It turned out that Coke stayed only six months in America before returning to England. Although he and Francis parted with heavy hearts, he would in the future only make brief visits to America, leaving the primary leadership of the new church to Francis. Except for the times when he was very ill, that was the way Francis liked it. Although he had great affection for Bishop Coke, he simply could not share leadership with anyone.

Before Coke left in June of 1785, however, he and Francis moved on two fronts. One was an effort to get slavery abolished, and the other was the establishment of a school.

When Thomas Jefferson wrote the original draft of the Declaration of Independence, he included a strong judgment against King George III for protecting the slave trade. The northern slave traders, however, supported the southerners in getting that statement removed from the final draft. All the colonies sanctioned slavery.

Francis hated it, as did Coke. As early as 1778 Francis had observed how Quakers were working for the liberation of slaves. *They should be praised for that,* he thought, *and Methodists must do the same work,* "or, I fear, the Lord will depart from them."

This was the one passion strong enough to involve him directly in politics. Although he and others sought strong antislavery stands among the Methodists, he knew that the church alone could not cope with this complex human issue. So he and Coke circulated petitions asking state legislatures to pass antislavery laws. They got the Virginia Methodist Conference in early May of 1785 to send a petition to the Virginia Assembly. Then they made a call on General George Washington at his Mount Vernon plantation, overlooking the Potomac River, maintained by his and Martha Washington's large number of slaves. They asked him to sign the petition to the Virginia Assembly. Washington did not sign it but said he would write the assembly supporting the petition if it came up for consideration by that body. In later years when Washington died in

1799, Francis noted that he was "a true son of liberty in all points" by ordering that his slaves be freed upon his death.

The sensitivity to suffering that Francis recognized in himself made it both physically painful and emotionally depressing whenever he was among slaves. He held worship services with them, urged masters to free them, worked for both governmental and church laws for their freedom. "If the Gospel will tolerate slavery, what will it not authorize!" he exclaimed. He could imagine nothing more contemptible.

Yet on into the future he would work for compromise between those who agreed with him and those who did not to avoid another possible split in the church. Nothing should destroy the Methodist connection. He laid himself on the line for unity no matter what the controversy. He tried to work, therefore, with both slaves and their owners in such a way that he could change attitudes of the owners without making them hostile to Methodism. If the church divided on the issue, he said, it would lose the opportunity to convince masters to liberate slaves. It always remained equally important for him to win everyone to Christ.

He was not timid, however, to speak out for what he believed. Later, when preaching in North Carolina, he wrote, "My spirit was grieved at the conduct of some Methodists that hire out slaves at public places to the highest bidder, to cut, skin, and starve them; I think such members ought to be dealt with; on the side of the oppressors there are law and power, but where are justice and mercy to the poor slaves? What eye will pity, what hand will help, or ear listen to their distresses? I will try, if words can be like drawn swords, to pierce the hearts of the owners."

In many Methodist societies both blacks and whites were members, often with blacks, even in slave-owning states, greatly outnumbering whites in their society. Racial tensions sometimes existed in the societies, however, and blacks eventually formed their own congregations in New York, Philadelphia, Wilmington, and Baltimore. Francis was their friend and their bishop as long as he lived. He ordained Richard Allen and Daniel Coker, two leading black ministers, and kept the congregations in full connection with the Methodist Church. It was only after his death that they separated into other denominations—African Methodist Episcopal, where Allen was named the first bishop, African Methodist Episcopal Zion, and other churches.

In education John Wesley had already set the pace for his followers in England. He had established schools, Sunday schools, and a book publishing operation. In the New World, the "Wesley of America" would do the same. Francis established the Sunday school movement among American Methodists with the beginning of one in Virginia. He also set up a Book Concern in Philadelphia to publish books and pamphlets.

Before the Christmas Conference of 1784, Francis had met Coke at Abingdon, about twenty-five miles from Baltimore, to look at a possible site for a school. They got the historic conference to approve the project. Coke sailed for England two days before the cornerstone was laid on June 5, 1785, for Cokesbury College, named for both bishops. The school opened its doors two years later to students.

Cokesbury College for Francis, however, was almost his undoing. For one thing, Cokesbury was an early experiment as a central school to be supported by all Methodists. But the average person did not have the money or the desire to support a school. Only the most wealthy, elite people in the country went to school.

Francis at times sounded as if he opposed even educated ministers. "It is said that there is a special call for learned men to the ministry; I presume a simple man can speak and write for simple, plain people, upon simple, plain truths." At other times he complained about preachers who had no interest in learning or reading. Although the ignorance of many preachers caused him pain, his standards were not as high as John Wesley's. As one biographer notes, "If only one could teach the rudiments, provide the books, and inspire the discipline to study, it would be enough."

The rudiments, or basics, included learning to read and write, which were taught to poor children, both white and black, in the Sunday schools. Reading profitable books, Francis said, kept one from being idle and took "off all the miserable listlessness of a sluggish life."

Most of all he wanted a boys' school for children of the preachers; he worried about them growing up with a father gone from home most of the time. The school would also be for orphans, and for those who wanted to become preachers. He remembered his childhood training and limited schooling. No doubt he hoped his efforts would make it possible for poor boys, such as he had been, to have the education of their dreams. Although he would be as strict with the school rules as with the rules to be a Methodist, one thing he would not approve: the whipping or striking of students. His vivid memories of his own cruel beatings by the schoolmaster at Snail's Green many years before would not allow it.

The rules Francis and Bishop Coke drew up for the school, however, were still severe. Providing strict religious training, Cokesbury would take boys as young as seven years old in order to have a longer time to form "their minds . . . to Holiness and Heavenly Wisdom as well as human Learning," Francis wrote. The children were to rise at five o'clock and be ready for morning prayers at six. The bishops said early rising was important to both the body and the mind. It prevented and removed "nervous complaints." It strengthened "various organs." It enabled "the mind to put forth its utmost exertions."

There was time for recreation during the day, but Francis and Coke set down what could be done during that period: "gardening, walking, riding, bathing" (limited to one minute in the water, and no bathing in the river!), plus working as "carpenters, joiners, cabinetmakers, or turner's business." Students could do no "play . . . for those who play when they are young will play when they are old."

There were requirements for every hour of the day. Studies were conducted for four hours each morning and three each afternoon. Subjects included English, Latin, Greek, logic, rhetoric, history, geography, natural philosophy, astronomy. "To these Languages and Sciences shall be added, when the finances of our College will admit of it, the Hebrew, French, and German Languages."

Since religious education was the highest priority, it was Francis's view that other subjects must not contain material to pollute children's minds. He questioned the content of many poems. He decided that "poets ought to be purged or burnt and not to be used in Christian schools." He, however, occasionally tried his hand at writing poetry. He showed some of his poems to his friend, Philip William Otterbein. "You was not born a poet!" was Otterbein's response. Francis went home and burned them all.

At seven o'clock, after supper, Cokesbury students were again in public prayer. Bedtime was nine o'clock, "without fail." Idleness was a fault deserving punishment, and the rules were strictly enforced.

Francis admitted later that Cokesbury's rules were too harsh. They were trying to "have the boys become all angels!" It was natural for Francis, however, to expect students to be as devoted as he to God and to work.

The school, though, was not thriving. It attracted no more than seventy students. Moreover, it was deeply in debt. Because Bishop Coke was out of the country most of the time, Francis was the main fund raiser. He also donated much of his sixty-four-dollar annual salary to the cause.

Later in 1795 when the school burned, Francis said, "Its enemies may rejoice, and its friends need not mourn! Would any man give me ten thousand pounds a year to do and suffer again what I have done for that house, I would not do it." Raising money for the school took time away from his main purpose for being in America.

Yet Bishop Coke wanted to continue the school. With some friends he raised enough money to buy a dance hall next door to Light Street Church in Baltimore. The church people and the dance hall owner did not get along. He had a habit of scheduling dances or concerts on the same nights the Methodists were singing and praying next door. "We American Methodists pray, and preach, and sing and shout aloud," said Francis. He called it holy noise. It would attract dancers from the hall to see what was happening at the church; this angered the owner to lose his paying customers. On the other hand, the Methodists did not appreciate the dance hall noises. What an answer to prayer to convert the dance hall into Cokesbury College!

The college prospered for several months in Baltimore. Then fire struck again and burned down both the school and the church. Francis felt that God was giving them a message. "The Lord

called not . . . the Methodists to build colleges!"
he wrote.

Cokesbury stayed closed after that. Francis
never again pushed for one school for the entire
church to support. He did help establish several
local schools organized by Methodists in the
geographical area. None of them survived many
years. Their strictness may have been a factor in
their failure. The largest factor however was that
the people were not yet interested in providing
money for the formal education of needy students. But by 1820, after the death of Francis,
Methodists decided that annual conferences
needed to support education. Their decisions
paved the way for the church in future years to
erect more than one hundred and fifty educational
institutions.

◆CHAPTER 9◆

TRAVELING
AROUND THE CONTINENT

◆

Francis Asbury and America were made for each other. People were on the move, and the Methodist bishop could be counted on to go right with them. While he was involved in attacking slavery and evil habits, such as alcohol, and establishing the new Methodist Episcopal Church and schools, such as Cokesbury, he was always traveling.

By the late 1780s he set up a travel schedule that began usually in January in Charleston, South Carolina, where he stayed for a few days or weeks each winter for his health. By 1788, his circuit north included crossing the Appalachian Mountains to the settlements along the Holston River of east Tennessee, then back to Virginia, Maryland, New York, and on into New England. He would then return in order to get back to South Carolina the next winter for its annual conference. All along the way he would hold quarterly meetings and annual conferences of the ministers in a geographical territory. Each conference would be expected to make decisions on the business of the church. It would take a year for him to make the rounds of the continent on horseback. And of course he would preach in homes all along the way. Wherever preachers were assigned, wherever there were people, wherever there was trouble, he would be there. Nobody could keep him away.

But how could he hold the church together over a territory of thousands of miles? That's where his talent for organization went into full swing and influenced the entire history of Methodism.

In each local church every group or class meeting had a leader. His duties were to schedule each week's meetings, keep tabs on the conduct of members, train the children, organize the class meetings to take care of the needy, and to bring others into the church. The traveling preachers, or circuit riders, could not do this kind of needed everyday work in any one location. Although assignments were changed by the bishop regularly, the circuit rider could be depended upon to make his rounds, preach, try to heal any tensions among the members, bring books to sell or give away, and share news.

Francis as bishop organized several of these circuits into a "district" with a preacher appointed to supervise the traveling preachers. These supervisory "presiding elders" (now called district superintendents) traveled around the circuits every three months and met with class leaders and preachers. They would also hold preaching and prayer services, serve Holy Communion, and hold a "love feast." Hundreds would attend.

In the middle of all this was Francis. His travels gave him the chance, also, to evaluate the work of the preachers so that he could properly assign them to the right place. In the 1780s he spent a great deal of time in the southern states of Virginia, the Carolinas, and Georgia for more than health reasons. Methodism was strong in the South, and he needed to do what he could to change attitudes about slavery. While there he also reestablished a friendship with Episcopal minister Devereux Jarratt, in Virginia. The two had been close friends since Francis's early days in Norfolk before the Revolution. Jarratt, one of the Church of England priests who worked closely with the Methodists in his parish, strongly opposed their forming an independent church.

Francis was eager also to go to the people over the mountain. As early as 1786 he crossed over from West Virginia and stepped foot in Ohio. By then he had organized a Kentucky circuit, and Methodists were already in the Northwest Territory by the time it opened in 1787.

His first trip into the forestlands of Georgia was that same year, as was his first conference in the Holston circuit of east Tennessee. He crossed the Appalachian Mountains from North Carolina to meet with the preachers assigned to Holston, West Virginia, and Pennsylvania. He rode his horse through mud and mire in the rough mountain passage, swam across creeks, and slept in abandoned shacks, only to ride perhaps fifty miles until midnight the next day before stopping again. Hideous screams of night owls, dismal howls of wolves, and shrieks of panthers filled the black nights with dread.

"We journeyed through lonely wilds where no food could be found except what grew in the woods. . . . Near midnight we stopped at William Anglin's, who hissed his dogs at us. . . . Our supper was tea. . . . I lay on a few deer skins with the fleas. That night our poor horses got no corn; and next morning they had to swim the Monongahela (River). After a twenty miles' ride we came to Clarksburg, and man and beast were so outdone that it took us ten hours" to get there. About seven hundred people attended the conference that year in Clarksburg.

Francis did not think too highly of the territory or the people who were not already Methodist friends. He thought the pioneers were adventurers who were far away from civilized society. Their warfare with "the savages," a common term for the American Indian in that day, taught them to be cruel, he said. He preached to "lifeless, disorderly people. . . . It is a matter of grief to behold the excesses, particularly in drinking, which abound here." In addition, how glad he would be to have a "plain, clean plank to lie on, as preferable to most of the beds; and where the beds are in a bad state, the floors are worse. The gnats are almost as troublesome here as the mosquitos in the lowlands" along the coast.

Yes, "this country will require much work to

make it tolerable," he said. It was just the kind of challenge he loved!

He had already named a presiding elder and seven circuit riders to the western region. These traveling preachers worked the area the same as those east of the mountains. "If they were welcomed," wrote one biographer, "they made Methodists of everybody in sight; if they were opposed, they did the same; if they were ignored, they did the same."

In late July of 1788 Francis went east, across the mountains into Pennsylvania, and got to Baltimore by August 10 for the conference. He had completed one of the longest journeys of his career and was exhausted. His "mind was clogged," he said, and could hardly take care of the business of the church and all the people who wanted to see him. The Baltimore event was his sixth conference that year in six different states. As soon as it was over he was off to Pennsylvania, New Jersey, New York, Maryland, and Delaware for the rest of the year. There were not enough preachers for the fast growth of the new church. He had to do everything he could to find more.

For those interested in preaching, the bishop demanded that they be willing to travel the circuit rather than settle down in one place to live. He did not want them to marry. Their first loyalty was to God, which under the Methodist system meant they must travel, and it was not fair to wives for their husbands to be away from home almost all year long. (There were no women ministers. It would be more than a hundred years after Francis' death that Methodist women would be given limited rights as ministers and a hundred and forty years—1956—before they could be ordained.)

To stay in one place, Francis thought, *followed the traditional Congregational or Presbyterian system*—"local, local, local, bishops and all! . . . the good man must stay at home, day after day, like other lazy priests," he would scornfully complain. He fought the movement toward a "local" preaching appointment all his life. How could preachers win people to Christ if they did not travel to them? A model for Francis went all the way back to Saint Paul in the New Testament, who was a traveling Apostle for Christ.

Preachers may have fought over the notion of traveling, cried about it, gone insane over it, or loved it; but under Francis they traveled. The weather could be terrible enough to draw the remark, "There is nobody out today but crows and Methodist preachers."

Sometimes preachers could take the strain only a few years. Several died young. Some married and located in one place as a lay preacher. Others dropped out of the ministry altogether. Sometimes they moved farther west and became a class leader in a new territory.

Every one of the preachers had to learn how to relate to their bishop. Francis was certainly an evangelist, always on the move to preach the gospel according to Methodist beliefs. Many claimed he acted like an unbending military commander. He clearly played the martyr, and his many illnesses made that easy. All these factors guaranteed that there were people opposed to what he was doing, but one control he would not give up was the assignment of preachers to their traveling circuits. John Wesley did it in England; Francis did it in America. It was the Methodist way, and he would not let anything about appointments even *appear* to be under someone else's control. That was the right of the bishop. One congregation asked Francis, for instance, to send them a particular minister. He did not. It would look as if the appointment were decided by the congregation, he said.

On another occasion a preacher by the name of James B. Finley wrote Francis requesting a circuit in the West near some of his relatives. At the conference when Francis read his appointment aloud, Finley was sent a hundred miles farther east than where he already was stationed. Afterwards he said to the bishop:

"If that is the way you answer prayers, I think you will get no more prayers from me."

Francis smiled and stroked his head. "Be a good son in the Gospel, James, and all things will work together for good."

Preachers who prayed for certain assignments, Finley said, were the most disappointed. "If their prayers were answered it would be against the prayers of the churches who pray to be delivered from them!"

Although preachers knew without a doubt that the bishop held the authority over where they would be sent to work, that did not mean they all liked it. It was said once that at the end of a conference, Francis would have his horse waiting at the door. As soon as he read out the assignments and gave a closing prayer, he would mount his horse and leave, without telling anyone where he was headed. If he could not be found, no one could argue with him over assignments.

One thing critics could never complain about— Francis demanded just as much of himself, if not more. He never asked anyone to do something he was not willing to do. He was leader of the Methodists in America, but he claimed no special treatment. "Born to govern," people said of him, but the new bishop did not look the part. For those who had never seen him, "we were led to view him," said a Tennessean, "as one living away in some great city, in a large house, and of wealth and power, and a kind of king."

Nothing was further from the truth. He kept his same plain frock coat, either light blue or gray, not buying another for more than a year until he wore it out or gave it away to a poor preacher. He owned one waistcoat and a broad-brimmed hat with an uncommonly low crown, and carried battered saddlebags thrown across the seat of a worn saddle. In his bags he carried Bibles, books, and pamphlets from the Book Concern to sell or give away.

His face was grave, his manner dignified, and his dark, heavy eyebrows made him look severe. His expression showed the intense devotion he gave to his task. He traveled all over America, some saying he missed not a single trail. He crossed the Appalachian Mountains in the coming years about sixty times. Occasionally he traveled great distances to lonely families on the frontier simply because he believed they had a right to know their bishop. People claimed they could count on him to make his rounds of the circuits as surely as the seasons came from year to year.

He survived torrential mountain rains ("In the mountains it does not rain, but pours," he said), worn-out horses, the southern swamps, and ticks and fleas that infested some of the log cabins where he endured a night's sleep. He often went into great detail in his journal over the physical hardships and indulged in defending himself against critics on the basis of his trials.

"I will make a few observations upon the ignorance of foolish men who will rail against our Church government," he wrote. "The Methodists acknowledge no superiority but what is founded on seniority, election, and long and faithful services. For myself, I pity those who cannot distinguish between a pope of Rome, and an old, worn man of about sixty years, who has the power given him of riding five thousand miles a year, at a salary of eighty dollars, through summer's heat and winter's cold, traveling in all weather, preaching in all places; his best covering from rain often but a blanket; the surest sharpener of his wit, hunger . . . ; his best fare, for six months of the twelve, coarse kindness; and his reward, suspicion, envy, and murmurings all the year round."

He traveled from Maine to Georgia, from

Kentucky and Tennessee to Ohio, and back to the middle coastal states. He considered it a personal insult to be delayed by illness, a weak horse, or bad weather. If he could be the one to bring even one person to Christ "in traveling round the continent, I'll travel round it till I die."

No less devotion did he expect from all the preachers.

◆ CHAPTER 10 ◆

THE WEST IS CALLING!

◆

At the New York Conference meeting at John Street Church on May 24, 1789, the preachers took time out from their church business to adopt a letter of congratulations to General George Washington. He had been inaugurated as the first president of the United States on April 30 in New York, following the adoption of a Constitution the year before. Bishops Asbury and Coke delivered the letter to the president on June 1.

It was the first formal congratulations of any church to the new head of government. This "event caused a stir in the city" and was written up in the newspapers. The Methodists who had been persecuted during the Revolution—with many of their members scattered to Canada and the West to save their lives—were showing, the news accounts said, that the "whole Society are warmly attached to the Constitution and government of the United States."

The letter to the president expressed confidence in his wisdom and integrity to preserve both civil and religious liberties and to "prove a faithful and impartial patron of genuine, vital religion." The president replied thanking the Methodists for their prayers and "demonstration of affection and . . . joy" over his election. He hoped he would not "disappoint the confidence which you have been pleased to repose in me."

The exchange certainly showed the hope of Methodists that the president would not try to limit the expression of religion or seek to have a government supported church. At the same time, it seemed to be a way of saying, "Let's lay down the resentment and bitterness of the Revolution against one another; we are now one people."

That was the ideal, but as Francis left the meeting with the new president, he knew that the ideal was far from a reality both in the church and in the nation. The country was squabbling over whether or not the states would have more power than the federal government. The church tension grew out of a move by a preacher, James O'Kelly, to limit the power of the bishop. But Francis would deal with O'Kelly later; he was now determined to go west. He had formed new circuits there he had not yet visited.

He left New York and headed west along the Forbes Road, one of two main routes pioneers took across the Appalachian Mountains in Pennsylvania. Pittsburgh was his destination, a small village of four hundred people. Although he had set up a Pittsburgh circuit, the village had as yet no preaching appointment. He evidently had other plans on his mind, too. From Pittsburgh he wrote a letter to Cornplanter, chief of the Seneca Indian nation.

The nation, living on the upper Allegheny River, had heard about the Methodists. Chief Cornplanter sent word that he wanted the bishops to send preachers to his people. Francis no doubt was fascinated by the idea. "I hope God will . . . send messengers to publish the glad tidings of salvation among them," he wrote. Why he did not help God by sending in preachers is not known. Certainly the Senecas lived in an area one hundred and fifty miles north of Pittsburgh that was controlled by hostile tribes. Massacres farther west had claimed many victims, some of them Methodists. Perhaps Francis simply found no one willing to go to a chief plainly calling for a missionary.

The next year Francis expressed real fear of hostile tribes. On his spring trip north from Charleston, he crossed the mountains from North Carolina to Tennessee, then over the old Wilderness Road to Kentucky for the first time. One of the preachers had written, asking him to come. He knew it would be dangerous, but he had stationed circuit riders in the territory. He would not refuse to go simply because the Indians were angrily resisting the thousands of pioneers crossing the trail into their lands. It was his duty to go, and swerving from duty was unknown to him.

Wherever he went in the mountains of east Tennessee and western Virginia on this trip, he stayed overnight where someone had been killed by Indians. Or the men in the family were hunting horses stolen by Indians. Or he heard stories of families killed or taken as prisoners, including two children of preacher Joseph Blackmore. Settlers often stationed a guard while they plowed their fields.

Before crossing into Kentucky, therefore, Francis and Richard Whatcoat, the presiding elder, formed an armed company of eighteen men to travel the Wilderness Road to Cumberland Gap, then across a narrow Indian trail. They traveled about fifty miles a day "over mountains, steep hills, deep rivers, and muddy creeks; a thick growth of reeds for miles together; and no inhabitants but wild beasts and savage men." Francis slept one hour the first night, two the last night; they ate no regular meal.

Along the Wilderness Road they saw graves of victims of the largest Chickamauga Indian massacre. Four years earlier twenty-four members of three families had been killed and scalped, and five women carried away. "These are some of the melancholy accidents to which the country is subject for the present; as to the land, it is the richest . . . I have ever beheld," Francis reported.

It was land several Indian tribes, including the Cherokees and Shawnees, would not easily give up to invading white people.

Francis and his traveling host, Whatcoat, felt pity for "the people in these backwoods." They also believed that many of them were wicked wretches and brought their own destruction down on their heads. They lived with their lives at stake every day, but "they seem to have no more religion than savage tribes."

One of the joys of the trip for Francis was visiting Charles White in Lexington. How many times Francis had eaten meals in his home in New York, where White had been a trustee of Wesley Chapel on John Street. During the Revolution White had stayed in New York while the British occupied the area, but as a Loyalist escaped to Nova Scotia after the war, then migrated west. So had another friend of Methodists, Frederick Deveau, whose manor north of New York was confiscated after the war.

During the weeks in Kentucky, Francis and Whatcoat held conferences and preached from farm to farm. They planned for a school, Bethel, near Lexington, which became the first Methodist school in the state of Kentucky.

He also moved among the people to set up class meetings. The frontier was both scary and lonely. Pioneers could come together in groups of ten or twelve according to the Methodist class meeting arrangement for prayer, for sharing one another's burdens, and for helping one another stick to their rules of behavior. While he was with them, he shared the burdens of both the preachers and members. They looked forward to his coming the next year and hundreds would come to hear him preach and pray. They remembered his kindnesses to them. They remembered the hardships he suffered to reach them, and they remembered his example and his message of God's love.

James Gwin, who moved over the mountains in

1791 and built a cabin about twelve feet square in east Tennessee near the Kentucky border, said the "holy men who risked their lives to come and preach to us had to be guarded from station to station; and while we would be guarding them from one preaching place to another, they would talk to us of Jesus and heaven and the things that belonged to our peace; and so strong and powerful were the attachments formed for them, that we would have died in their defense."

On this first trip into Kentucky, Francis was very pleased over the number of people who were brought to Christ. He also remembered their warm affection. He had been "blessed among these people, . . . I would not, for the worth of all the place, have been prevented in this visit, having no doubt that it will be for the good of the present rising generation." He knew the rising generation would get larger and larger in the West.

He had a responsibility, however, for the rest of the continent so he headed back across the Wilderness Road. About fifty had joined him, twenty of them armed for protection of the group. Francis was cautious. He drew up an agreement that each one in the company must sign to abide by the rules; they must stay together at all costs if attacked. Those who would not sign were left behind.

Although they discovered signs of Indians and thought they heard voices, they kept traveling fifty miles a day for three days and were not attacked. By June 2 they reached McKnights on the Yadkin River in North Carolina. "Here the conference had been waiting for me nearly two weeks: We rejoiced together, and my brothers received me as one brought from the jaws of death."

Two years later when Francis again braved the wilds of Kentucky, he had about the same experience as in 1790. At one of the stations where the company stopped along the Wilderness Road, "we found such a set of sinners as made it next to hell itself," he complained. No doubt they were playing cards, drinking, dancing, swearing, and laughing. The miserable conditions of the trip made him so ill that he was certain he would die.

When he got to Bethel School near Lexington, he changed the plans of the house so that the students would be more comfortable in cold weather. He wrote letters to promote the school, held conferences and public worship, preaching one to three hours at each place. The western parts had suffered because of his absence, he thought. But "I . . . hear so much about Indians, convention, treaty, killing, and scalping, that my attention is drawn more to these things than I would wish." While there, an alarm was spread about an Indian raid near the settlement. He was so afraid when returning along the Wilderness Road that rather than sleep, he "walked the encampment and watched the sentries the whole night. . . . We had the best company I ever met with—thirty-six good travellers and a few warriors; but we had a pack-horse, some old men, and two tired horses."

While he was often afraid on these trips and shared the common attitudes of pioneers about Indians, he could grasp the situation of the tribes. They had also been massacred by white people and were enraged over the invasion into their hunting lands. And many, such as the Wyandots in Ohio, were peaceful, settled farmers from many generations back. A difference in Francis' view from the common notions about Indians was that he regarded them not as "varmints" but as people who needed to be saved by Christ. In a short time Methodist missions would be started among them. And when the United States Congress passed the infamous Removal Act, which forced Indians to move west of the Mississippi River in the 1830s, Methodist missionaries would move with them—especially with the Wyandots, Cherokees, and Shawnees.

◆ CHAPTER 11 ◆

THE KEY TO THE CONNECTION

John Wesley died in England in April of 1791. At that time Francis reviewed all Wesley's accomplishments in his eighty-eight years and concluded that the "dear man of God" had no equal "among all . . . he has brought up."

Bishop Coke, who had just arrived in America two months earlier, rushed ahead to sail again for England after they heard the solemn news. Although Francis had held the Founder of Methodism in high respect and affection, he had come to America more from what he believed to be a call from God rather than only an assignment by Wesley. Because of the distance and the views of people in the New World, Wesley certainly never had complete control over Methodists in America. But the new church, which was formed at the 1784 Christmas Conference, would select as part of its doctrine, or views about God, the writings—sermons, notes, and minutes—of John Wesley; and his pamphlets and tracts would not go out of print in America. They went along with the Bible in the saddlebags of traveling preachers.

Francis said he would never read Wesley's works without reflecting on the loss which the Church of God and the world had received by his death. But Francis did not return to England. He stayed in his adopted country and named preachers to the circuits for the coming months.

He may well have wished he could have consulted Wesley over the O'Kelly controversy, which came to a peak at the first General Conference held on November 1, 1792, in Baltimore.

James O'Kelly, a preacher in Virginia, hated the power Francis had as a bishop, not just in assigning preachers, but also in how he conducted the business of the church in conference meetings. He called Francis a tyrant, even labeled him as one of the horns of the seven-headed beast mentioned in the book of the Revelation in the Bible. But the best way to get at the bishop, he decided, was to limit his authority over the assignment of preachers to their circuits. If a preacher did not like his assignment, O'Kelly suggested, he could appeal to the conference. If the conference agreed with the preacher, it could ask the bishop to change the assignment.

Francis knew ahead of time what O'Kelly would try to do. He also knew what O'Kelly and friends thought of him. Better to be thought a tyrant, he decided, than to be viewed as a weakling with no sense of duty. He strongly opposed O'Kelly's proposal. Appointments of preachers then could be appealed over and over again if he as the bishop were restricted by such a plan.

He dreaded the debate. He must have brooded and prayed over how the first split in the church could be avoided. He had no desire to listen to arguments that would limit his power, particularly if there were the chance he would lose the vote. Since Bishop Coke was back in the States, he turned the conference over to him to preside. Francis went to the home of a friend. He had a good excuse; he was terribly ill.

The debate raged on for two days and many of the preachers stood with O'Kelly on limiting the bishop's power. Then Francis sent a masterful letter to the members of the conference. It drew sympathy for the ailing bishop, and made them question the wisdom of O'Kelly's proposal. The kindness in the letter completely disarmed them.

When the vote was taken, a large majority supported Francis. O'Kelly was a poor loser. He pulled out of the church and took several pastors and several thousand members with him to organize his own church. He remained a bitter foe of Francis for several years.

The main unity of the church had been preserved despite the pullout by O'Kelly and his supporters. Francis could not be bothered with continuing to fight over issues; there were more important works to do for God. He was more concerned about the unity of the church than he was in O'Kelly's personal bitterness; he would not direct anger toward O'Kelly. So at the conference he noticed that O'Kelly, who had been a preacher for several years, was "almost worn out." He suggested that the Methodists continue to give him a pension each year. Since O'Kelly needed the money, he accepted it for about six months.

After the conference ended Francis headed south on his regular rounds, which would bring him eventually back to Charleston. He heard along the way that some groups were leaving the Methodists to join O'Kelly. It was disturbing to him, but he said, "If we lose some children, God will give us more." Despite this attempt at being objective about it, O'Kelly caused him pain for many years. Meanwhile, people on his southern journey were coming out, he said, in great numbers to "hear this man that rambles through the United States."

Perhaps Francis thought O'Kelly might come back into the church if the Methodists had compassion for his financial needs. O'Kelly did not. But Francis did not give up on two other ministers who left with O'Kelly—Jesse Lee and William McKendree. He simply appointed them later as his traveling companions; he would win them over while working with them day in and day out. His strategy worked. They came back into the Methodist Church rather soon, and McKendree would be named a bishop in 1808. In the end, almost all the "O'Kellyites" returned to the church.

By the mid-1790s his travels into New England were well established each year. Francis had formed circuits in New England, but he felt his own visits there held little success. Religion was seemingly well established with a Congregational Church in each community, but he noticed little fire for the faith. He could not understand why people did not flock to the Methodists after hearing one of their preachers. The New Englanders' lack of overwhelming response saddened and irritated him, but he would not give up on them. If they would just pray constantly, he was sure God would work wonders among them.

So Francis continued during the 1790s: building churches, raising funds for schools and support of preachers, ordaining ministers, baptizing new members, writing letters, organizing the church, sending preachers into new circuits, and working with John Dickins, whom he had named to head the Book Concern in Philadelphia to publish materials both for preachers and members.

He even rode into port cities like Philadelphia during outbreaks of yellow fever. Over four thousand died in Philadelphia within a two-month period in 1793. Valuable members of the Methodist Church died or fled the city; Francis could not stay away.

The yellow fever scare spread throughout the states. Francis said it was the sins of the people that had brought God's wrath on them. He preached sermons on the theme, "Search and try our ways and turn again to the Lord." The people of God he said would know God's judgments and profit by them. They would turn from their wicked ways. In those days many people tried to explain the terrible things that happened to them in this way: God was punishing them for some evil they had done. Francis had been taught that from childhood. He would preach it till he died.

The next year he was so ill that he decided if he went west across the mountains, it would probably cost him his life. He sent word that he would not meet the conferences. He stayed longer in Charleston that winter and preached, read, received visitors, wrote letters, held quarterly meetings, and fell into "gloomy melancholy, the worst I've had for several years."

The next winter, 1795, he did the same. It was best not to think about distressing subjects, he wrote. His depressions came more often when he was ill and when he stayed in one place where he had more time to think. It was as if he would have gone mad if he could not keep traveling. "To move, move seems to be my life," he said.

Once when so ill he could not sit up but felt he must not delay his journey another hour, he had his companions strap him to his horse so he would not fall off. The physical abuse he put his body through seemed to be more desirable than the melancholy of his mind. The depression was "deeply constitutional," he decided, and would not go away until he died.

At those times he brooded over the terrible behavior of people and their unwillingness to hear the message of God. He also brooded over the good Methodists who were staying away from services and class meetings; over masters who would not listen to appeals to liberate blacks and who ridiculed those preaching liberation. He also brooded over his own unworthiness of God's favor, and his lack of living completely for God, which must be the cause of his pain and suffering. His constant sense that he was not worthy of God's love kept him from being a harsh dictator in the church.

By 1796 when Francis was fifty-one years old, his health was bad enough that he began to worry about retirement. Who would be bishop in his place? Although he was unhappy over his slower pace and his inability to take the hard travel of his younger days, he could not imagine himself in a retirement of "honor and ease." If he did, "then farewell to religion in the American Connection System," he said. He was the key person to keep the traveling connection going, he felt. There was always work to do, so he must be doing it. Some part of God's cause might suffer if he did not thrust himself into his work each day. But he admitted he could no longer ride and preach as in former days. He therefore agreed to ride more in a carriage than on horseback.

But "live or die, I must ride." He set out north again in February of 1797 with the blessings of his friends and particularly one black woman about ten years older than he. She supported herself in Charleston by picking oakum to make rope. Yet she wanted to give him a gift of money, a French crown. "She had been distressed on my account, and I must have her money," he wrote. "No! Although I have not three dollars to travel two thousand miles, I will not take money from the poor." Her gift was a symbol of how much her bishop meant to her.

Francis was able to make it over the mountains to east Tennessee that year. "My horse has the honor of swimming Holston River every time I visit this country," he said. But some of the preachers talked him into putting others in charge of conducting the next Kentucky and Cumberland conferences so he would not have to do it. He "traveled six hundred miles with a fever and fixed pain in my chest."

Eventually he ended up at the Perry Hall, the manor of his good friend Mr. Gough, where he regularly stayed when in the Baltimore area. He assigned Jesse Lee, presiding elder and the key leader of Methodism in New England, to conduct the New England conference for him. He worried more over the need of a bishop to take his place. Americans should act as if they were going to lose him any day, he said. So he asked the Virginia conference for advice in November; its members suggested he rest until the same conference in April of 1798. He appealed to Britain to send Bishop Coke back: "We have only one worn out superintendent and he needs rest." William McKendree was assisting him now, but Francis began preparing everyone for the fact that at the General Conference of 1800 he would resign as bishop—if he lived that long.

Francis did not go to Charleston that winter. He could not bear to ride ten miles. "It depresses me to think I may die by inches," he said. He took carriage rides out across the countryside on occasion when he felt better, and worked on his journal and other publishing interests of the Book Concern with John Dickins. Many days, however, he could only pray, wind cotton for the women of the household, and listen to someone read to him.

By April he was back on the road visiting the circuits in all the northern states all the way to Maine. That fall a yellow fever plague hit Philadelphia just as it had the previous year. Ninety people a day were dying in the city; one of them was his close friend, John Dickins, head of the Book Concern.

Francis also received word in May that his father had died in England. The long years away had erased his memory of his parents' faces, but he could well remember their love. How fortunate to have them for parents, he said, rather than the king and queen, or any of the great. He had not returned to see them simply because of his single-minded mission to America. The people he served needed him, he had often told his parents, and the work would suffer if he were away. In fact, he thought he would be sinning against God and the church if he went back to his homeland.

Moreover, he did not want his parents to come to America. It would give him great pain if anything happened to them at sea. He remembered his voyage as a time when his health problems had begun. And once here they would be disappointed in seeing him so seldom because he was here and there and everywhere on the continent. He simply had to forget his own country and his father's house; he must die in America. Besides, if they had come over they might not be so holy as they ought to be!

Before his mother died in 1802, he reminded her in a letter of a scene from his childhood. "You used to say, 'Frank, you will spoil your eyes.'" But her warning would not take him away from reading the Bible by twinkling firelight. Surely the story helped her understand how little he had changed from his early training.

CHAPTER 12

CAMP MEETINGS IN A WILD LAND

On they came over the Appalachian trails, floating down the Ohio River—twenty thousand people a year pouring over the mountains to migrate west. Some of them came, it was reported, with their fiddles, packs of cards, and pistols. Others came barefooted, struggling on bleeding feet through the passes. Others drove their small herd of hogs and cows, riding scrawny ponies. By 1800 when the Wilderness Road was wide enough for wagons, they swarmed from the east—all seeking a patch of land of their own, a land they thought was flowing with milk and honey.

"There were four or five hundred crossing the rude hills while we were," Francis noted once. "I was powerfully struck . . . that there were at least as many thousand emigrants from east to west: we must take care to send preachers after these people."

In most cases, the preachers were there to meet them when they arrived. Three who made the journey through Cumberland Gap in 1800 were Francis, Richard Whatcoat, and William McKendree on their way to the first meeting of the western conference in Kentucky. It was that year that Francis discovered the camp meeting.

He had not resigned at all at the General Conference in Baltimore. Granted, he had been so ill that he didn't expect to live to see the turn of the century, but since he had it was not in his nature to let go of the work. His self-sacrifice to establish the church in America and carry it forward would be discounted if he lived a retirement of ease and nursed his ailing body. If he were going to let his poor bones have top attention, he would have retired at the age of twenty-six. It could not be called living to sit in his room all day, making gloomy reflections on the past, present, and future life.

Besides, the General Conference (which had been meeting every four years since 1792) did what he asked them to: they elected another bishop, Richard Whatcoat—always referred to by Francis as "assistant" bishop. If Francis died on the road, at least he had the satisfaction that the church had another leader to carry on. By the end of the conference he was feeling healthier than he had in months.

The conference also helped out the poor preachers by increasing their yearly allowance from sixty-five dollars to eighty dollars and requesting circuits to provide homes for them. Francis hoped this would keep so many preachers from dropping out of the ministry.

That was also the momentous year that Francis appointed young William McKendree as presiding elder of the western district, the only district in the western conference. He was well suited to the rough and raw frontier, and would spread Methodism from the mountains to the Mississippi River.

A native of Virginia, McKendree took the challenge of the West with the same devout commitment that Francis had taken on America. And when he came to the General Conference of 1808 and preached before all the ministers in Methodism with a powerful enthusiasm, Francis noted that his sermon would get him elected bishop. Francis was right. McKendree was elected bishop that year to join in the sacred work with Francis, "the old father in the faith."

After the conference of 1800, however, Francis had his mind on the West. This time he traveled with Whatcoat and McKendree to Nashville, Tennessee, for the first time, and preached to more than a thousand people for over three hours. The next day they came upon a camp meeting the Presbyterians were holding for several days at Drake's Creek meetinghouse.

It was the first camp meeting of many that Francis would attend in the next fifteen years both west and east of the mountains, for once he discovered them he encouraged them wherever he went. Camp meetings were perfect opportunities for Methodist preachers. Methodists had been preaching outdoors ever since the movement had begun in England, anywhere they could gather two or more people. At the camp meetings people would in coming years attend by the thousands for two or three days, perhaps a week or more. "This is fishing with a large net," Francis noted.

At camp meetings Methodists could preach to larger audiences and organize class meetings. They could even hold their annual or quarterly conferences at the same time. But most of all they had a wide audience for their message of free salvation from God. You did not have to earn your way into God's love by your actions, they said. Ask God for forgiveness of your evil ways and you can know that he has forgiven you and live by that faith. Your heart can be changed, they said, but when it is you will then live by strict rules to seek perfection before you die. And you will tell others that God can save them, too. How could you not share this good news as long as there was even one person who did not know about Jesus Christ?

People came on foot, horseback, carriage, or wagon from as far as fifty miles away to the camp meetings, which were usually held in a grove of trees near a spring. They brought their own food and pitched their hunting tents in a row or circle. Behind the tents were the wagons where the men might sleep underneath and the women and children inside. Behind the wagons they tied and fed the horses.

Trumpets would call people at dawn to rise and call them to preaching services all during the day and night. They built altars in several places on the grounds, and often ten to thirty ministers would preach at the same time.

Evening services might go on for several hours, with the grove lit by candles, lamps, torches, and campfires in the still night. Hundreds of people wandered around, some preaching, others praying, shouting praises to God, singing, or sharing their sorrows and joys with one another. Those who felt the presence of God and were confident he had forgiven their sins would "fall like corn before a storm of wind." They would then go off with their friends and neighbors to a quiet spot in the woods or to a wagon or campfire and try to win them to Christ.

Such excitement for religion did the heart of an old bishop good. Francis received cheering accounts in years to come from letter writers across the continent about the huge numbers they were receiving into the church at camp meetings. He was sure that Methodism would thus grow and spread to the Pacific Ocean, to South America, "and all the Floridas, French and Spanish, if the work goes on." He wanted the continent and the world to flame, he said, with the spiritual glory of God.

The zealous, noisy Methodists, as he called them, could not help but do good wherever they went. As he traveled his heart would go out to the people in the small New England settlements where he preached in the woods, in homes, and in chapels. He shared with them their most common meal, a broth with pork and cornmeal mixed in, and hasty pudding. He wept over their misery—a part of the country where village paupers' auctions sold poor widows, orphans, or old, handicapped people to the lowest bidder for cheap labor—as much as he wept over the misery of the slaves. Some of those may have tried to escape their misery to join the throngs going over the mountains.

Francis might find them in the wild country of Ohio, where he headed after his New England schedule. There wildcat skins hung on the wall of the one-room log cabins, wild turkeys' wings were stuck in the cracks. Whether the cabin was neat and clean or filthy, Francis would receive a smiling welcome. He would put his hosts at ease so they forgot their embarrassment over entertaining a bishop, and he shared their meals of milk and mush, occasionally a bit of wild meat, and coffee made of toasted cornbread.

On every trip he stayed with some families who were complete strangers. They immediately became friends even though it was strange to have someone preach and pray with them. Most likely he would arrange to come back by the home to preach again and ask them to gather in everyone from the countryside. Thus everywhere along the roads and trails he could stay most of the time with friends who loved him dearly and expressed it with their kindness and in weeping when he left. Many years before, Madame Russell in southwest Virginia, for instance, had enlarged her house to take care of people when Francis came to visit. The sister of Patrick Henry and widow of General William Russell, she received Francis regularly on his trips across the mountains. She and her husband were also two who freed their slaves after they became Methodists.

"During the last few years of Asbury's life his travels through the domain of Methodism were triumphal processions," wrote one biographer. "He was by now the best known man in the United States, and wherever he went great crowds assembled to see him and hear him preach. He was entertained by mayors and governors, and when he visited a capital city during a session of the legislature, he was invited to address the statesmen. . . . Methodists throughout America . . . regarded him with awe and veneration, and it was not uncommon for a congregation to burst into tears as he tottered or was carried into a church." At camp meetings he was known to calm a rowdy crowd simply by standing in their presence. Thousands, both young and old, claimed him as their spiritual father.

Meanwhile, he kept his eye on the expansion of Methodism, which was taking place primarily in the West. "It is wonderful to see how Braddock's Road is crowded with wagons and packhorses carrying families and their household stuff westward—to the new state of Ohio, no doubt," he wrote in 1804. "Here is a state without slaves," and better for poor, hardworking families. "O highly favored land!"

Into that land he placed a preacher who went on to become a famous circuit rider in the West, including Indiana and Illinois. Peter Cartwright was won to Christ in a camp meeting in 1801 and given a certificate to preach the next year. He was seventeen years old.

At the conference in Kentucky in 1806, Francis ordained Cartwright. The bishop often told his preachers, Cartwright reported, that "You read books, but I read men." With his penetrating blue eyes, he could look right through someone "as if you had a window in your bosom; he could see what was there." Others noted that he looked into the character of a person as one looks into a clear stream to discover the bottom.

At the western conference of 1806, Francis was giving a good hard look at Cartwright. By the end of the conference he would have to make the assignments of preachers to their circuits. He would sit with his eyes half-closed, watching the preachers and listening to them, sizing them up, and deciding where they were to preach the next year. He probably studied Cartwright well and heard reports of his work. He knew that Cartwright could take the hardships of the Marietta circuit in Ohio, where the provincial government of the Northwest Territory had been located. As it turned out, he was right, but Cartwright did not think so.

The Marietta circuit covered one hundred and fifty miles and he had to cross the Ohio River four times on every round of the circuit.

"It was a poor and hard circuit," he wrote. "Marietta and the country round were settled at an early day by a colony of Yankees. At the time of my appointment I had never seen a Yankee, and I had heard dismal stories about them. It was said they lived almost entirely on pumpkins, molasses, fat meat, and bohea tea; moreover, that they could not bear loud and zealous sermons, and they had brought on their learned preachers with them, and they read their sermons, and were always criticizing us poor backwoods preachers. When my appointment was read out, it distressed me greatly. I went to Bishop Asbury and begged him to supply my place, and let me go home. The old father took me in his arms, and said, 'O no, my son; go in the name of the Lord. It will make a man of you.'

"Ah, thought I, if this is the way to make men, I do not want to be a man. I cried over it bitterly, and prayed too. But on I started . . . ."

The preachers knew that when Francis took them aside to pray privately with them, he was going to assign them to a hard place.

CHAPTER 13

. . . UNTIL THE DAY HE DIED

By 1808 the territory had grown into a vast region. The westerner Cartwright reminded Methodists much later that there were no steamboats, no railroad cars, or comfortable stagecoaches. Preachers would take a month to travel by horseback each way to the General Conference each four years; and while they were gone those three months the Baptists would try to win over their members!

For the first time, therefore, the conference decided to elect representatives, one for each five members in each annual conference. The representatives would make the decisions for the whole church. This kept every minister from having to make the trip to the General Conference.

The conference also elected William McKendree as the first American born bishop. Bishop Whatcoat had died in 1806, and for two years Francis had carried the responsibility alone. "The burden is now borne by two pairs of shoulders instead of one," said Francis. "The care is cast upon two hearts and heads."

During the conference, its members also set aside their work for the funeral of Harry Dorsey Gough whose home at Perry Hall near Baltimore had been the meeting place for Methodists since the days of the Revolution. More than two thousand heard Francis preach a funeral sermon on Gough's contributions to God's work.

With the election of another bishop, an ordinary man might have given up the work. Instead Francis continued his annual tours to all the conferences. He traveled with Bishop McKendree; in addition, Henry Boehm traveled with them as assistant to Francis. Then John Henry Bond was his assistant the last two years before Francis's death. The people expected them to come in season. Francis believed the respect and affection people had for him was due to his regular presence among them. "Are we riding for life?" he asked. "Nay! But we must not disappoint people; we are men of our words."

But in fact he was riding for life. He continued to care for the preachers. He raised money right up to the end for their support. Preachers who were in desperate situations at annual conference frequently received his shirt, hat, or coat right off his back, sometimes even his watch. And he willed his two thousand dollars of savings at his death (which had been willed to him by friends) for pensions to the preachers.

When meeting earlier in Tennessee in a large upper room of a home, Francis asked John Adam

Granade to leave while the conference decided on whether or not to approve him as a preacher. When he was called back in, Francis said to him, "We are raising money for a destitute preacher. How much will you give?"

Granade took out his purse and gave it to the bishop. "I have two dollars. Take as much of it as you want."

Francis took Granade's purse, added his own money to it, plus the money he had already collected from the others. Then he handed it all to Granade and hugged him with affection. "You've been approved as a preacher," he said. "The money is for you."

Francis never changed his mind about married preachers. To do God's work and travel as they did, he was as convinced as ever that they should remain single. At a Baltimore conference in 1809 when he made the offhand remark, "I would not give one single preacher for a half dozen married ones" one married preacher after another stood and resigned.

Francis had tripped himself. "What did I say?" he asked, startled. When told, he said, "Did I say that? . . . Well, forgive me, I will say it back."

"Then, sir, we withdraw our resignations!"

Neither did age change his mind about the control of the bishop to assign pastors. He no longer walked out when he disagreed with proposals at conference as he did in the O'Kelly struggle of 1792. Now he simply turned his back on the speaker as if he were not listening. At the 1812 General Conference Jesse Lee was appealing for preachers to be elected to the position of presiding elder. This was another attempt to limit the bishop's ability to appoint them.

Francis showed his opposition by facing the wall and sitting with his back toward the speaker and the preachers in the audience. In his view, it was poison for preachers to try to win votes from one another.

After Lee's strong argument was near conclusion, another preacher said, "No man of common sense would have advanced such arguments."

Jesse Lee replied, "Our brother has said no one of common sense would use such arguments. I am, therefore, Mr. President, compelled to believe the brother thinks me a man of *uncommon* sense."

Francis must have enjoyed the humor in that. He wheeled around to face him. "Yes! Yes! Brother Lee, you *are* a man of uncommon sense."

With quick wit Lee replied, "Then I beg sir that *uncommon* attention may be paid to what I say."

But Francis turned again to face the wall. The preachers got a good laugh out of it, and Lee got to finish his statement. But his proposal was defeated by the conference.

Even after Francis was violently ill in 1814 for three months, he pushed himself throughout the states for his appointed rounds of all the conferences. "I look back on a martyr's life of toil, and privation, and pain, and I am ready for a martyr's death," he said, crossing the Appalachian Mountains again into the western conference. Some days he was too weak to preach or pray or conduct the conference. But he was there. And his presence gave a holy atmosphere, it was said, to the gathering. It was as if he could be counted God's faithful servant in his own mind only if he were on the road. From early days he had sung the verse,

> In hope of that immortal crown
> I now the cross sustain
> And gladly wander up and down,
> And smile at toil and pain.

By September of 1815, Francis was seventy years old, had completed the rounds to South Carolina, as far north as Massachusetts, and was back in Ohio. Both he and Bishop McKendree were present for the Ohio conference, which began its meeting on September 14 in Lebanon.

The patriarch of the church, with his long flowing white hair and trembling limbs, still urged the church to wider frontiers. Francis was not content to see the church grow from its six hundred or so when he first arrived in America to the present two hundred and fourteen thousand members and seven hundred preachers. He wanted to call missionaries over from countries where German, French, and Spanish were spoken so that Methodists could better reach the immigrants pouring into the country; and he was organizing circuits in the southwest—Alabama and Mississippi.

When he preached, it was said, his words moved the people as the trees of the forests were moved by a mighty wind. "If I had a thousand hearts and tongues and a million of years to live, all would be insufficient for paying the mighty debt of praise" to God, he said.

"Bishop Asbury, in very feeble health, was not able to walk or stand alone," reported Jacob Young, presiding elder of the Ohio district. "The Rev. John Bond . . . carried him in his arms like a little child, set him in his carriage when he wished to travel, and took him out in the same way when he wished to stop. . . . He prayed as if speaking to God face to face. . . . I saw that Asbury's work was done, and that he was going home to God. He was truly . . . sent of God on a special mission to these United States. He had done his work, and done it well. Although the Methodist Church had many great and good teachers, she had but one father under God, and that was Francis Asbury."

The worn and wasted old man, coughing all night with consumption, had traveled over nine hundred miles since June 1 and had preached every week. He planned with Bishop McKendree how the West should be divided into five conferences. He traced outlines and boundaries for the church's territory. Then he moved on with his companion, Bond, to Kentucky, Tennessee, and North Carolina to arrive in South Carolina in December. The last entry in his journal of more than forty-five years was on December 7, 1815: "We met a storm and stopped at William Baker's, Granby."

By then, America had ended its second war for independence against England, called the War of

1812. The country was on a more certain path. The Methodist Episcopal Church, too, was passing from a sect to a church, less dependent on the personality and work of one man—their rambling bishop.

More like a "walking skeleton than like a living man," Francis determined that he should go to the General Conference in Baltimore on May 2, 1816. Baltimore was like his center and his home. If all the preachers were going to gather, he must be with them.

Stopping to preach at several places along the way, he arrived in Richmond, Virginia, where he preached his last sermon on March 24. Bond carried him to the pulpit and set him on a table in the old Methodist church. He preached for more than an hour, often stopping for long pauses to catch his breath. His message was like the last words of a dying father to his children.

He then traveled for three more days before arriving on Friday evening at the home of an old friend, George Arnold, in Spottsylvania where he was taken from his carriage for the last time. He called together the family on Sunday morning for a service of worship where Mr. Bond sang, prayed, and preached. The Bible passage from the lectionary for the day was in the book of the Revelation:

"And God shall wipe away all tears from their eyes; and there shall be no more death, neither sorrow, nor crying, neither shall there be any more pain: for the former things are passed away."

Francis remembered the preachers to the end. He asked for an offering to be received for the most poor among them, and Bond reminded him that only the family was present for the service.

As he sat in a chair later in the day, he died with his head cradled in the hand of his young faithful traveling preacher, Bond, whom he had ordained. He died contented that he had never let go of his calling from God. The date was March 31, 1816.

Bond sent a messenger to Methodists across the continent. "Our dear father has left us. He died as he lived—full of confidence, full of love. . . ." He did not have to call the dear father by name.

His body was taken to his beloved city of Baltimore and buried during General Conference on May 10 in a vault under the pulpit of the Eutaw Street Church. Thirty-eight years later it would be moved to Baltimore's Mount Olivet Cemetery.

The funeral procession was headed by Bishop McKendree, followed by the preachers of the General Conference, ministers of other denominations, and a representative of the British Methodists. More than twenty thousand mourners marched through the streets of Baltimore.

"I live in God from moment to moment," was one of the last entries Francis had made in his journal. Other than that assurance, he would have cherished most the throng of traveling preachers in America from north and south and east and west who attended his funeral.

◆

SACRED
to the memory of
THE REV. FRANCIS ASBURY,
Bishop of the
Methodist Episcopal Church.
He was Born in England, August 20th, 1745;
Entered the Ministry at the age of seventeen;
Came a Missionary to America, 1771;
Was ordained Bishop in this city December 27th, 1784;
Annually visited the Conferences in the United States, with
much zeal; continued to preach the word
for more than half a century;
and literally ended his labors with his life,
near Fredericsburgh, Virginia,
in the full triumph of faith, on the 31st of March, 1816,
aged 70 years, 7 months, and 11 days.
His remains were deposited in this vault, May 10th, 1816,
by the General Conference then sitting in this city.
His Journals will exhibit to posterity his labors, his difficulties,
his sufferings, his patience, his perseverance,
his love to God and man.
His remains were again removed from this vault, and deposited,
by order of the General Conference of 1852, in a
cemetery near Baltimore; and a monument
is raised to perpetuate his memory to
future generations.

◆

◆ BIBLIOGRAPHY ◆

Quotations used in this book are from Asbury's journal and sources listed in this bibliography.

Asbury, Herbert. *A Methodist Saint: The Life of Bishop Asbury*. New York: Alfred A. Knopf, 1927.

Bayne-Powell, Rosamond. *English Country Life in the Eighteenth Century*. London: John Murray, 1935.

Bennett, William W. *Memorials of Methodism in Virginia, 1772-1829*. Richmond: Published by author, 1871.

Boatner III, Mark Mayo. *Encyclopedia of the American Revolution*. New York: David McKay, 1966.

Bucke, Emory Stevens, general editor. *The History of American Methodism*. Vol. I. Nashville: Abingdon Press, 1964.

Carpenter, Allan. *Ohio: From Its Glorious Past to the Present*. Chicago: Children's Press, 1963.

Cartwright, Peter. *Autobiography of Peter Cartwright*. Nashville: Abingdon Press, 1956, Centennial Edition.

Caruso, John Anthony. *The Appalachian Frontier: America's First Surge Westward*. Indianapolis: Bobbs-Merrill, 1959.

Christensen, Gardell Dano, and Eugenia Burney. *Colonial Delaware*. Nashville: Thomas Nelson, 1974.

Church, Leslie F. *The Early Methodist People*. New York: Philosophical Library, 1949.

Clark, Elmer T., Editor. *The Journal and Letters of Francis Asbury,* 3 vols. Nashville: Abingdon Press, 1958; London: Epworth Press, 1958.

Clark, Thomas D. *The Rampaging Frontier: Manners and Humors of Pioneer Days in the South and the Middle West.* Indianapolis: Bobbs-Merrill, 1939.

Duren, William Larkin. *Francis Asbury: Founder of American Methodism and Unofficial Minister of State.* New York: MacMillan, 1928.

Earle, Alice Morse. *Home Life in Colonial Days.* Middle Village, N.Y.: Jonathan David Pub., 1975. Reprint of 1898 edition.

Feeman, Harlan L. *Francis Asbury's Silver Trumpet: Nicholas Snethen.* Nashville: Published by the author, 1950.

George, Mary Dorothy. *England in Transition: Life and Work in the Eighteenth Century.* Baltimore: Penguin Books, 1962.

————. *London Life in the Eighteenth Century.* New York: Harper & Row, 1965.

Gill, Jr., Harold B. and Ann Finlayson. *Colonial Virginia.* Nashville: Thomas Nelson, 1973.

Griffith, George W. *Francis Asbury: Founder of American Methodism.* Los Angeles: Mrs. G. W. Griffith, 1939.

Hyde, Ammi B. *The Story of Methodism.* Springfield, Mass.: Willey and Co., 1888.

Ingraham, Leonard W. *An Album of the American Revolution.* New York: Franklin Watts, 1971.

Isaac, Rhys. *The Transformation of Virginia, 1740-1790.* Chapel Hill, N.C.: University of North Carolina Press, 1982.

Larrabee, William Clark. *Asbury and His Colaborers,* vol. 1. Cincinnati: Hitchcock and Walden, 1852.

Lawson, Don. *The American Revolution: America's First War for Independence.* New York: Abelard-Schuman, 1974.

Loeb, Jr., Robert H. *New England Village: Everyday Life in 1810.* Garden City, N.Y.: Doubleday, 1976.

McFerrin, John B. *History of Methodism in Tennessee,* V. I. Nashville: Publishing House of the M.E. Church, South, 1888.

Norwood, Frederick A., Editor. *Sourcebook of American Methodism.* Nashville: Abingdon Press, 1982.

————. *The Story of American Methodism: A History of the United Methodists and Their Relations.* Nashville: Abingdon Press, 1974.

Rudolph, L. C. *Francis Asbury.* Nashville: Abingdon Press, 1966.

Smeltzer, Wallace Guy. *Bishop Francis Asbury in the Making of American Methodism.* Paper, presented May 19, 1971, Session of Northeastern Jurisdictional Commission on Archives and History of The United Methodist Church, Alexandria Bay, N.Y.

Stubenrauch, Bob. *Where Freedom Grew.* New York: Dodd, Mead, 1970.

Thompson, Edward P. *The Making of the English Working Class.* New York: Pantheon Books, 1964.

Tipple, Ezra Squier. *Francis Asbury: The Prophet of the Long Road.* New York: Methodist Book Concern, 1916.

Tunis, Edwin. *The Young United States 1783-1830.* New York and Cleveland: World Pub., 1969.

Wakeley, Joseph B. *Heroes of Methodism.* New York: Carlton and Porter, 1856.

Ward, Christopher. *The War of the Revolution.* 2 vols. New York: MacMillan, 1952.

Wood, James Playsted. *Colonial New Hampshire.* Nashville: Thomas Nelson, 1973.